THE CALL TO SERVE
The Thomas Mann Jr. Story

THE CALL TO SERVE
The Thomas Mann Jr. Story

By Senator Thomas Mann Jr.

The Call to Serve
Copyright © 2021 by Senator Thomas Mann Jr.

Content Editor: Maegan Daquano
Copy Editor: Mackenzie Eldred
Editor-in-Chief: Kristi King-Morgan
Formatting: Amanda Clarke
Cover Artist: Kristi King-Morgan
Assistant Editor: Maddy Drake

Printed in the United States of America

ISBN- 978-1-947381-43-8

www.dreamingbigpublications.com

To my wife Leala, my daughters Nari and Kari, and my extended family. This is a story about me and us. I've enjoyed living it and writing about it, and I hope you enjoy reading it.

Many people aided me in the development and writing of this book. I want to acknowledge the assistance of my eldest daughter, Nari Mann, for her encouragement. I also want to thank Diana Ceres for her work in shaping the manuscript.

I want to thank and acknowledge the editorial staff at Dreaming Big Publications for their work on the script. Specifically, I want to thank Maegan Daquano for her work on the content, Mackenzie Eldred for her work on the copy, Amanda Clarke for her work on the formatting, and Maddy Drake for overseeing the editorial process. Their work is greatly appreciated. Finally, I want to thank Kristi King-Morgan for her efforts in seeing this matter to fruition. All are appreciated.

The ultimate measure of a man is not where he stands in moments of comfort and convenience, but where he stands at times of challenge and controversy.
—Martin Luther King Jr.

Table of Contents

Foreword

Thomas Mann, Jr. is living a remarkable life, overcoming significant obstacles to serve the law and the common good. He has done it all with extraordinary goodwill, grace, and conviction.

Tom served two stretches in the Iowa Attorney General's Office, one before I was attorney general and once during my tenure. He was exactly what we were looking for in an assistant attorney general—able and ethical with a sense of public service, all in large amounts.

He worked diligently, representing the Department of Social Services. He was an example of how to treat others, both inside the office and outside. His book lays this out in a clear and inspiring way.

We were proud to see Tom leave us to pursue elected office and go on to serve two terms in the Iowa Senate. Tom served his constituents well while holding multiple leadership positions.

Racism took a toll on Tom in many ways, including physical and mental health problems. He is extraordinarily open about this in a way that's helpful to readers. He made difficult, but good, decisions about these challenges. This is another way Tom serves as an inspiration.

Reading this book is a warm, rewarding experience. In it, we see how Tom respects others, does the right thing, accomplishes the public good, and struggles successfully. These are important lessons, especially today. Indeed, more of us should feel the call to serve.

Tom Miller, Attorney General for the State of Iowa,
July 2019

Introduction

Time begins the healing process of wounds cut deeply by oppression.
— Rosa Parks

Rules and Codes

"When you boys are out, if you meet a white person, I want you to cross over to the other side of the road. Don't look them in the eye. They could take that as a challenge. And if you see a white woman, don't stare. It will lead to misunderstandings. And above all else, don't say nothing to no one unless spoken to. Do you hear me?"

I took a deep breath and looked over at my Uncle Alfred who was a few years older than me. He seemed unfazed. This was old hat to him. Lynchings of black men were not a secret to my grandmother. She lived in an apartheid world. She knew what could happen to a black child who challenged a white male, or who looked upon a white woman with favor.

I glanced over at my younger brother Jack and my cousin Yogi who were in the room with us. Their eyes were steady as they looked over at the family matriarch, Carrie Maclin, who was seated near the fireplace in her favorite chair, punctuating each rule with a creak of her rocker.

We all nodded in unison, "Yassum," as she handed my uncle the money. I looked over at Uncle Alfred as he stuffed the bills into the front pocket of his jeans. One day I would get to carry the money. I was looking forward to that day. My grandmother cleared her throat, causing me to look up. We all watched as she reached into her apron pocket and took out a near-empty bottle of Levi Garrett #3 snuff. She'd told me earlier that she was about out and that she needed Al and me to go to the store. Since I was about six or seven, which was old enough to pick cotton, she said I was old enough to tag along with Uncle Alfred and run errands for the family.

She studied us closely as she rocked. Satisfied that we understood the gravity of her message, she opened the bottle of snuff and deposited the remainder of finely ground tobacco into the palm of her left hand. She inhaled the tobacco and then looked directly at us, "You come straight home. We need you out in the fields later."

"Yassum," we nodded. Uncle Alfred turned to leave, and I followed his lead. Jack and Yogi gave my grandmother a pleading look, asking permission to tag along, but she shook her head and pointed to the kitchen. There was work to do. Disappointed, they headed into the kitchen, rolling up their sleeves, as Al and I headed for the front door. I was the last one out, so I closed the door quietly behind me and headed down the front steps of our three-room log cabin. It was a bright day, and I shielded my eyes at first as they adjusted from the dimness of the cabin.

This wasn't the first time my grandmother sent us to the store or ran the rules by us on the way out. We often went to pick up provisions like fryers and cornmeal and white fish and rice. These items were relatively inexpensive and could feed a large family. And while it's been over sixty years since she first uttered those words to me, they still haunt me to this day.

Growing up in the Jim Crow South in the mid-fifties was a challenging time for all African Americans. Even though slavery had been abolished with the 13th Amendment on December 6th, 1965, we were enslaved in other ways, such as the unspoken rules my grandmother reminded us of before we were allowed to head out into the societal landmine of our segregated community. A community that carried with it an undercurrent of racism and fear. The tension created by the oppressor and the oppressed was so tight, at times, I felt it would snap. My family and I tried not to disobey these rules because we knew that you could be beaten up, jailed, spat upon, or hanged with just one wrong move that defied the unspoken code of deference to the white man.

I remember once my grandfather, Floyd Maclin, brazenly disobeyed the code when we were out working in the fields. My grandfather used curse words as if they were a sword. He was formidable, and we tried to stay out of his way whenever he was angry. On one occasion, he let his anger override his common sense, and he cursed our landlord, who may have been one of J.B. Warren's sons, over a dispute while picking cotton in front of the other workers, some of whom were not members of our family. We were all on pins and needles for about three weeks after his outburst.

It was a dangerous time for my grandfather and for us. If our landlord had responded in the expected manner, other than cursing my grandfather back, we would have been evicted or worse. My grandfather could have been beaten or killed without so much as anyone giving it a second thought. Or us being able to dispute his actions by seeking legal justice for his death or our eviction.

Fortunately, our landlord may have been too ashamed for getting into a cursing match with my grandfather to do anything other than yell back. I talked about it with my Aunt Suzette while we were out in the field witnessing the events. She was just as alarmed and scared as I was.

J.B. Warren & Sons

"Hurry up!" Al yelled. I was lagging behind, thinking about my grandfather and the chores we had to do when we got back. I could tell it was going to be a hot day with not much of a breeze.

There were fifteen of us living in that small cabin. My parents, Thomas and Flossie Mann, had divorced when I was around two years of age. Soon after, my mother, brother Jack, and I moved in with her parents who also shared their home with my cousins and aunts and uncles.

We lived out on a country road in Haywood County, Tennessee. We were sharecroppers and raised cows, mules, hogs, chickens, geese, and turkeys. We also grew cotton and corn and tended to the animals and crops. In short, we did all the work, bore half of the expenses like seeds and feed, and received half of the proceeds. This was about as good as it got back then for a family in our position.

Al waved at me to catch up. There would be time to think about the chores when we got back. I ran to meet up with him as we took the three-mile trek to J.B. Warren's, a local store in Browns Creek. We didn't have a car, so we walked pretty much everywhere, even to school.

"What took you so long?" my uncle asked as I walked alongside him in the field. I shrugged my shoulders, "I was just thinking about Grandpa and how he was lucky he didn't get whooped by Mr. Warren." "The old man lucked out," Al chimed. "Don't you get no ideas, now. You might not be so lucky."

I nodded and held my head low as we walked through the cow pasture. It was getting hot and part of me wished we could ride to the store in an automobile like the white folks did. Al hated walking, too, and he was quick to mention it. At least it wasn't raining today. And we didn't see any white people on the way this time, so we didn't have to cross to the other side of the street like Grandma told us we had to.

When we got to the store, we were careful not to speak to any of the white folks. We also stuck close together and held our items out in plain view to avoid being accused of shoplifting, something I still do to this day, partly out of habit and partly because I'm often being eyed suspiciously because of my skin color. We knew the lay of the store by heart and carefully selected each item on my grandmother's list. When I wasn't looking, my uncle also picked up a plug of Cup chewing tobacco for us to try on the way home. He was mischievous like that.

When we got out of the store, he turned to me as he peeled back the wrapper on the chaw. "Just take a bite like this and chew it," Al demonstrated by taking a small bite and chewing. I was eager to take a bite. Maybe it would taste good. I was starting to get hungry, so I made sure it was a big one. Once I bit in, I made a funny face. Al laughed and told me I'd get used to it and motioned me to follow him home. As I chewed, I noticed the juice was burning the inside of my mouth pretty bad. I didn't care for the taste and decided I should just hurry up and finish chewing it before things got worse.

Al didn't swallow the juice but neglected to tell me. Pretty soon he spat out his chaw, but I wasn't paying attention because I was looking at one of the cars parked on the street and wondering what it would be like to ride in a car like that. Distracted, I swallowed the entire wad and then ran after my uncle to catch up. By the time we got back to the cow pasture, I was drunk beyond compare and started to wretch. When we got home, Al sent me straight to the fields so my grandmother wouldn't see me in such a state. It was one of the worst afternoons of my young life, but it cured me from ever wanting to try chewing tobacco ever again.

A Better Way

Over time, I grew envious of the privilege white people had and the luxuries they were afforded. They had comfortable housing, cars, nice clothes, and the ability to ride public transportation and to look people right in the eye when they were talking. Even though I knew of the unspoken rules, I had not often seen them on public display since we lived in a more rural community. I only saw it when the landlord would stop by to talk to my grandfather and I, and the other children would be sent to a separate room.

When I was in the fourth or fifth grade, and old enough to tag along, my grandfather would hook up the mules to the wagon and he and Alfred and I would go into Brownsville. This would be a Saturday shopping trip or a trip to the cotton gin in Nut Bush, Tennessee. On these occasions, I noticed the water fountains and restrooms and certain establishments all labeled with signs that read "Whites Only" and "Blacks Only." I came to accept these conditions without questions and unknowingly. At home, we were taught to be meek and accepting of the Jim Crow laws and social customs, but I started to realize something was very wrong with the way minorities were treated in this country, particularly in the South, and I wanted to do something about it.

From watching TV and reading newspaper reports, I came to believe that lawyers were the decision makers. I knew that if I was going to make a difference and pave a better way for other minorities, I needed to be in a position of power, too. By the time I was in high school, I knew that I was going to be a civil rights attorney and a politician.

My family was not in a position to support my education, however. We were struggling to make ends meet as it was. When I talked about going to college, no one objected, but I knew I would have to get in on my own merits with a scholarship and work odd jobs to pay for any other expenses. When I told my grandmother that I wanted to become a lawyer and a politician, she joked, "Why do you want to be a liar?" I smiled and told her this was how I could help the most people, and she nodded, approving of my decision.

While the path I chose was not an easy one, especially after being raised to be meek and deferential to those in positions of power, it was both a necessary and rewarding one. In the pages ahead, you will learn of my struggles as well as my successes as I acclimated to life after Jim Crow and worked to become a civil rights attorney and state legislator. There have been positive changes in race relations in the past fifty years, both socially and politically. In 1964, the federal civil rights act was adopted. In 1965, President Lyndon Johnson issued Executive Order 11246 requiring federal contractors to take affirmative action when hiring minorities. In 1965, the voting rights act was adopted. In 1968, the federal act prohibiting housing discrimination was adopted. These changes in laws prompted some changes in conduct, if not in mind. The "Whites Only" signs were taken down. In some places, desegregation began to occur. These were positive changes.

Unfortunately, at times, it seems as if we are treading water or even slipping backwards. While public schools are no longer legally segregated as they were when I was growing up in Haywood County, they are de facto segregated due to the residential boundaries created by the school districts. Women of all races and creeds continue to make less than men and still do not have equal rights in this country. And to this day, blacks can't go into a department store without having store security following them around accusingly. Police officers continue to shoot black men with impunity, and Hispanic children at the border are used as political pawns and separated from their parents to create a smokescreen to deflect from other events that reflect poorly on the current president. A president who fails to condemn the violent actions of white supremacists and refers to women as "pigs," Mexicans as "rapists," and his former black aide who criticized him recently in a memoir as a "dog."

Recent events underscore the unfortunate fact that we have many miles ahead of us in the fight to achieve social, economic, and political equality for minorities in this country. As I shared with my senate colleagues in January of 1985, "Let us today rededicate ourselves to the task of achieving Dr.

King's dream. And let us build a lasting monument to his memory by resolving today to work to accomplish the goals that he gave his life for. And like a tree, let our commitment take roots, and survive, and grow, and produce the fruits of justice, equality, peace, and freedom, for all Iowans, all Americans, and indeed, all humankind."

Thomas Mann, Jr., Manor, TX, August 19th, 2018

Chapter 1

A Bird in the Hand

We may have all come on different ships, but we're in the same boat now.
— Martin Luther King, Jr.

Silent Protests

"Move!"

I looked up and saw several football players climbing the bleachers in the school gymnasium. They were all headed my way. One of the players had his sights on me and was already standing over me. I looked around. There was plenty of room for them to sit. Why should I move?

"Did you hear me, boy? I said MOVE!"

I froze. The giant football player narrowed his eyes and stomped on the bleachers to make sure I understood his position as his teammates sat down on the bleachers within arm's length of me. Why did I have to come to the basketball game by myself? I should have waited for Bell. He said he wanted to come, but I was still sore at him for yelling at me.

I admit almost getting us shot last night wasn't the smartest thing in the world to do, but I wasn't thinking clearly at the time. We were all pretty upset, and emotions had been running high all week. Still, he came down pretty hard on me, and I wasn't feeling up to his company yet.

1

Don't get me wrong. I liked my roommates, Lebron Wright and Anthony Bell. We all got along famously. Bell was tall and gangly, and he usually kept us laughing. And on more than one occasion he let me bum a meal from his meal booklet since I was pretty hard up for cash back then. And Lebron was a good guy from Chattanooga. We weren't in any of the same classes at Tennessee State University (TSU), but we hung out whenever we could between classes.

On weekends we'd all go to the Omega Psi Phi parties and drink spiked punch from twenty-gallon garbage containers. And sometimes we'd go to the Wigwam, a local pub near the university, where we'd go shoot pool and hang out with other members of our fraternity. Once, I even got arrested for being in a "disorderly house." But that wasn't my fault. The owner of the pool hall didn't have a business license and a fight broke out, which drew attention to the establishment. It was one of those situations where I just happened to be in the wrong place at the wrong time. Fortunately, my dad came and bailed me out, so I didn't have to stay at the holding cell in the police station for long.

While I was attending TSU, my dad and I had rekindled our relationship. I saw him every few weeks. He'd always give me five or ten dollars whenever he visited, which I appreciated. Unfortunately, he'd also give me advice, which was less appreciated, but I never said anything. I'd just nod and keep my opinions to myself. And that went double the night he came and bailed me out. To his credit, he didn't say anything to my grandmother about the arrest. She would have been furious with me, and I know I would have gotten an earful when I went home to visit that Christmas had he shared any of it with her.

Overall, I had a good experience in college. Even though the legalized segregation of schools ended in 1954, the South, in particular, was slow to change. As a result, I attended all black schools through high school. And I remember seeing "Whites Only" and "Blacks Only" signs in public buildings well after Jim Crow ended. It wasn't until the Civil Rights Act passed in 1964, which prohibited discrimination on the basis of race, creed, color, and national origin, that the signs started to come down. Unfortunately, the prejudices and resulting injustices have remained.

TSU was the first unsegregated school I had attended, and I was a little apprehensive about how that would go. I chose TSU over Union University because it was a historically black college and many of my West High classmates were also going there. I guess part of me wanted to be around familiar faces. I knew I'd be going home for holidays and such, but this was the first time I would be out on my own, so I opted for an environment that would be a little more familiar to me.

It didn't take long to settle in. I had enrolled full-time and initially my attendance and grades were pretty decent. In the evenings, my roommates and I would listen to Dr. King's speeches on the radio. His words moved us, and I was especially motivated by all the civil rights work he was doing. He helped shape my views about politics and the issues of the day, which led me to join the Student Council so I could start making a difference on campus. Bell could mimic Dr. King perfectly. After listening to the speeches, he'd pretend he was Dr. King and start quoting him. He'd have me and Lebron in stitches every time he said, "I have seen the mountain top" and "They sicced the dogs on me!"

But that night none of us were laughing. It was April 6th, 1968. Martin Luther King, Jr. had been assassinated in Memphis a few days prior, and rioting had broken out throughout the country as the country protested the violent loss of a great leader and civil rights activist. The presiding Governor of Tennessee, Buford Ellington, was afraid students might riot at my school, so he had the National

Guard come out to make sure things didn't get out of hand. And he was right in doing so as there had been accounts of students talking about taking to the streets to protest Dr. King's assassination.

The administration had asked all the Student Council members to visit the dormitories to encourage students not to riot. We hit every dorm, including the women's freshmen dorm, to encourage everyone to keep the peace. By nightfall, Bell and I were back in our room. The Guard had been patrolling the campus. Soon after we got back, we heard some windows being shot out of a nearby building. I looked out our window at Watson Hall and saw a team of guardsmen standing watch about three hundred yards away. Just then, I remembered Bell had brought back some magnesium filament from the lab. I walked over to his dresser and picked up the filament and pulled a pack of matches out of the top drawer. I wondered aloud what would happen if I held the filament up to our third-floor windows.

Before Bell could tell me what a stupid idea that was, I lit the filament with a match and held it up to one of our windows. It blazed like a fuse. I waited for a while, but nothing happened. For a second, I was disappointed. I wanted to matter. I wanted all of us to matter. I didn't want Dr. King's death to be in vain. I wanted to be seen. Heard. Even if it meant risking my own life. I shrugged my shoulders and sat down on my bed, and I heard Bell let out a sigh of relief. As soon as I lay across my bed, however, the shots rang out, and both of our windows exploded. I held my breath as I watched glass shatter all across my bed.

When the firing stopped, I turned to my side and looked at my roommate. "Are you OK?"

He glared back at me. "Jesus, Tom. You could've gotten us both killed!"

Bell was pretty peeved, and he had a right to be. He shook his head and inched farther away from the window, in case more bullets were on the way. I looked over at the clock on my nightstand beneath the window. It was one of those wind-up clocks that made that loud "TICK TICK" sound every second. Even though it was on its side from the explosion, it was still keeping time. Bell and I held our breaths as we counted each TICK of the clock until we finally decided it was safe to move. I don't know how long we waited. It seemed like hours, but it could have been minutes. We were both pretty shaken up over it.

"The Guard is going to come in here and get us. You know that, right?"

I looked over at Bell. He had inched himself way into the corner of the room and was dusting off bits of glass from his bed. What a mess. It was going to be hard to clean up all this glass. Plus, I'd have to explain about the windows so we could get them fixed. I wasn't looking forward to any of that.

I hung my head low and nodded. "I know."

"Is that all you have to say?"

I shrugged my shoulders. What else could I say?

A few minutes later, I tried apologizing to Bell, but he wasn't having any of it. We kept waiting for the Guard to come, but no one knocked on our door. Once he realized we weren't getting arrested, he stormed out of the room and slammed the door behind him, but not before telling me what an idiot I had been.

Bleachers and Burlap

"Are you deaf, boy?"

Still reeling from the events of the week, I looked directly at the football player and said nothing. He wanted my seat, but I didn't feel like moving. I'd gotten there early to get a good spot and didn't think it was fair to just give him my seat just because he was bigger than me. Some of the other players had sat down near me and were trying to watch the game, probably hoping I would just scoot over and be done with it. Like provoking the National Guard, standing up to a giant football player probably wasn't in my best interest. These were big players, six to seven feet tall and well over two hundred pounds. And here I was, just five feet, seven inches and barely one-hundred-seventy pounds. But I held my ground all the same, determined to keep my seat.

The agitated player was about to take a shot at me when one of his teammates stood up and got between us. "Leave him alone. If you have a problem with it, you can take it up with me." The bully just shook his head and stormed off, leaving a rumbling in the bleachers in his wake.

I nodded my thanks to the player who had just stood up for me. I watched as he waited for his teammate to leave before he sat down again. It was Claude Humphrey who saved me from getting beaten up, and I was forever grateful to him. After that, I followed his professional career with the Atlanta Falcons. Because of his kindness toward me, he became my favorite professional football player. And even though my homeboy from Jackson, Tennessee, "Too Tall" Jones was sitting right next to him and said nothing that night, I followed his career, too, and enjoyed watching him play with the Dallas Cowboys. Whenever I watched their games on TV, I thought of that night and was thankful I'd been spared.

My roommate Bell eventually forgave me, but it took some time to patch things up. And in spite of the high tensions on campus that week, there was no rioting. Later that week, the governor had asked the Guard to leave, and life soon returned to normal for us on campus. At the time, I was pretty active with the Student Elections Commission and my fraternity. My grades took a bit of a dive after I joined the

Omega Psi Phis, though. The parties were a lot of fun, and they kept me up late, which cut into my studying time.

I was also working full-time making burlap bags at Werthan Bag Company in Nashville from 11:00 p.m. to 7:00 a.m., which also cut into my sleep time. So, I started skipping my morning classes to catch up on my sleep and began timing the production cycle at the plant so I could take short naps while the burlap bags wrapped around the spools. When my fraternity brothers found out I was skipping classes, they told me I had to start going to class if I wanted to stay in the fraternity. Faced with a tough decision, I learned how to cultivate more balance in my life by attending parties on weekends, sleeping in class during the week, napping during part of my shift at work, and studying enough in between to make passing grades.

I also joined the Political Science Club, which led to my participation in the Tennessee Intercollegiate State Legislature (TISL). I knew this would be good practice for the future I wanted in legislative politics. During these annual legislative sessions, students from across the state visited the Tennessee Capitol Building in Nashville and offered legislative solutions to the problems facing the state. I really enjoyed these sessions where I was a parliamentarian tactician. I studied the rules applicable to this legislative activity and laid out the legislative strategy for my classmate Robert Hunt to argue on the floor. I knew what motions to make and when to make them. Learning Robert's Rules of Order also came in handy with my role as parliamentarian for the Omegas at TSU and later on as a state legislator.

My senior year, I started applying to different law schools, including the University of Iowa in Iowa City and Carnegie Mellon University in Pittsburgh. My final grades at TSU were fair. I finished with a 2.94 grade point average and graduated with a bachelor's degree in political science in August of 1971. I was determined to attend law school before taking a job or getting married because I didn't want to be tied down with work or a family before I could pursue a career in law and politics.

Iowa City

I was accepted to several law schools but chose the University of Iowa because they had the best financial aid package. I didn't know anything about the state. If I had known more about its demographics and climate, I might have chosen another school. At the time, Iowa's minority population was about four percent. And, as I later learned, it gets very cold in Iowa during the winter.

The summer after graduation, I began preparing to move to Iowa. While my family depended on us to help with the farming, they were thrilled that I had been accepted into law school and fully supported my decision to further my studies. My cousin, Wayne ("Yogi") Maclin, who later became a preacher in Des Moines, agreed to loan me his car to drive out there. But first, we had to put a motor in it.

My great uncle Buddy (Booker T. Maclin) loaned me fifty dollars so we'd have gas money for the trip. He also provided the new motor for Yogi's car. My brother Jack, Wayne, and I figured out how to install the new motor. It was a 1964 Chevrolet Impala. It was easier to put a motor in a car back then, as cars did not have computers. Unfortunately, we didn't have enough money to buy new tires. The ones on Yogi's car were dangerously bald, so we always drove carefully to avoid getting into any accidents.

In August of 1971, Jack and I started driving toward Iowa. We drove through St Louis, Missouri, and then proceeded on to Iowa. The closer we got to Iowa, the "whiter" it became. Jack and I began to feel uneasy as we drove through the middle of Missouri and into Southern Iowa. We were both about twenty years old and from rural Tennessee where people did not travel out of state since it was an agrarian economy. So, we were a bit uncertain about venturing into areas where there were fewer black faces. In spite of our apprehension, we drove on until we reached Iowa City.

By the time we arrived, we were pretty nervous. In 1971, Iowa had a small minority population, which included African Americans, Hispanics, and Native Americans, and we weren't sure how we would be received. Given the fact that we grew up in the rural South during the Jim Crow era and were taught to avoid white people, it left a general sense of uneasiness in our stomachs. Fortunately, the people we met (both black and white) were friendly and helpful.

I sent my brother Jack back to Tennessee with the car after we found an apartment in town near the university. It was a small first-floor efficiency with convenient access to the bus stop. Since I didn't have a car initially, I relied on public transportation to get around, which worked out OK since Iowa City has a pretty decent bus system. My first week there I registered for my classes, picked up my financial aid packet, and got settled in.

Law school took some getting used to. They do not use the traditional teaching methods I was accustomed to. Instead, they use the Socratic method to teach their students. This method requires that professors question students about particular fact patterns, which gives students the opportunity to learn from themselves and each other. The professors also do not generally answer students' questions. I was not familiar with this method but fancied myself a pretty good student. According to my professors, however, I wasn't, as I finished law school with a "C" average, in stark contrast to graduating top of my class at West High School back in Denmark, Tennessee.

But I can't really blame my law school professors. After my first semester, I stopped attending classes on a regular basis. I'd worked hard, but my grades weren't reflecting the amount of effort I was putting into my classes. I guess I decided if I wasn't going to get good grades, I should stop working so hard. While I did spend some late nights studying for my classes, I was more focused on the political activities on campus. I served as president of the local chapter of the Black American Law Students Association (BALSA) and was the black student union representative in the student senate. In addition to serving as a member of the Board of Trustees of Student Beneficial Services, Inc., I cofounded the Mu Delta chapter of the Omega Psi Phi Fraternity with twelve of my fraternity brothers across campus, where I served as cofounder, treasurer, and president.

Friends and Family

Halfway through my first year of law school, I decided I needed a car. I called my mom, and she put me in touch with my Aunt Watie Ruth and Uncle Sylvester in Chicago who were interested in selling their car. For $300 cash, I bought their 1968 red and black Pontiac Bonneville convertible.

Now that I had reliable transportation, I decided to move a little farther from campus. I found a three-bedroom apartment in Coralville and invited my best friend, Larry Grimes, to come up from Tennessee and live with me. It was nice having a friend around, but I was starting to miss my family, too. So, after a while, we decided to invite my Uncle Alfred to come live with us. Soon after, I invited my brother Kenneth and my cousins Jesse and Robert, whom I recently saw at my Aunt Watie's funeral. I loved having a full apartment. It reminded me of the small cabin and close quarters I lived in when we were growing up in Tennessee. While I attended school, they worked at Sheller Globe, the veteran's hospital, and the University of Iowa doing an assortment of jobs, ranging from maintenance work to janitorial and assembly line type work.

We ate a lot of Hamburger Helper in those days. Alfred was a good cook, but his work schedule kept him pretty busy, so I took on a lot of the cooking duties and made a lot of quick, simple meals. In our spare time, we'd hang out at some of the local pubs in Iowa City. We played pool at Joe's and The Pub. Whenever I needed to catch up with my classes, I'd spend hours late into the night reading cases and studying in the law library where it was quieter. I must have studied enough because I managed to graduate with a juris doctorate degree in the spring of 1974.

A Bold Move

I was planning to return home after law school and set up a law practice in Tennessee. But sometimes life has a way of deciding for you. After graduation, I went to Des Moines and holed up in a room at the Kirkwood Hotel to study for the state bar exam. I crammed night and day for about three weeks straight. I was nervous about taking the exam because I was a mediocre student and had not attended all of my classes. However, all the last-minute studying must have paid off because after three grueling days of testing, I found my name on the list posted by the exam proctor and learned that I'd passed.

At the time, it was the duty of the attorney general of Iowa to offer the motion for the new graduates to be admitted to the state bar. Richard Turner was the state attorney general in June of 1974. I remember he came to the Hotel Fort Des Moines where the admission ceremonies were being held and offered the motion.

Afterward, I remember standing on the sidewalk in front of the hotel with one of my law school classmates, Lewis Martin, and his friend, who had also just passed the state exam. As Attorney General Turner approached us, Lewis whispered, "Ask him for a job!"

I looked at Lewis like he was crazy. I couldn't do that. Besides, I was planning to go home and practice law there. Before I could refuse, however, Attorney General Turner was standing right in front of us, asking what we were going to do now that we'd passed the state bar. My classmates were quiet. Lewis elbowed me, and the next thing I know, I'm clearing my throat and asking the state attorney general of Iowa for a job.

"I don't have a job yet, but I was hoping that you'd give me one."

Attorney General Turner smiled, probably thinking I was joking. Heck, he wasn't far off, as I hadn't planned any of this. What was I doing? Before I could chicken out, though, Lewis interjected, "I think Tom would be a real asset."

I looked over at Lewis, who nodded, encouraging me to continue.

"I'm, uh, interested in civil rights law and the cases your office is handling. I, uh, served on the Student Council at TSU and was president of BALSA here at the University of Iowa."

Attorney General Turner nodded as I added more confidently, "I think I have a lot to offer and would really like the opportunity to work for you."

The attorney general studied me for a moment, considering my proposal. In that instant, I was back on the bleachers in the TSU gymnasium. A mysterious force kept me locked on that sidewalk, looking back at Attorney General Turner, refusing to back down as I had once done when the football player asked me to move. Determined to get that job, I stood in front of him until he finally said, "Well, why don't you follow me back to my office so we can have a proper interview?"

I agreed and immediately drove to his office at the state capitol. As I was following him, I kept thinking, "A bird in the hand is worth two in the bush. You may want to go back to Tennessee, but here's a job. A good job right here. Go get that job." While I never planned to stay in Iowa after I graduated from law school, much less embark on a political career there, I'd set everything in motion that day by asking General Turner for a job.

During the interview, Attorney General Turner had asked me whether I was a Republican or a Democrat. I realized this was a pivotal question. One that had to be answered carefully. While I knew I was leaning Democratic, I replied that I was not a card-carrying member of any political party. General Turner was a Republican and could probably tell from my enthusiasm about civil rights that I was a Democrat. However, he was satisfied with my careful response and hired me on the spot, fresh out of law school, to be an assistant attorney general of Iowa.

When I left his office that day, I took a deep breath and looked out over the city. It was time to look for an apartment in Des Moines.

Chapter 2

Lessons and Litigations

Pick your battles.
— North American proverb

Johnny Lee's Farm

I'd been working for Richard Turner, the attorney general for the state of Iowa, for a few months now. The work was interesting and new. Prior to that, I had no real interest in practicing criminal law, but I found it interesting once I'd started working for Turner. My loyalties, however, lay with my family and my home state of Tennessee. So, while I was working for the attorney general, I had gotten permission to take the Tennessee Multistate Bar exam in Memphis.

About two weeks after I'd taken the exam, I'd spoken with my grandmother Carrie Maclin on the phone. She'd advised me that she had received a letter from the State Bar stating that I had passed the exam. I was thrilled to hear this and was starting to think about when I'd like to return home. Just a few nights prior, I was even planning a trip back home to start scouting office locations.

After getting home from a pretty busy day at work, I thought some more about moving back to Tennessee. It was hard not to grow excited about the prospect of practicing law and helping folks in my home state. I was about to make some dinner and just relax at home for the night, but before I could open the refrigerator, the phone rang.

I walked over to the wall phone by the kitchen counter and picked up.

"Hello?"

"Tom, is that you?"

It was my grandmother Carrie. I was surprised by her call since we'd spoken just a few weeks ago, and we weren't in the habit of talking that frequently. While I had passed the state bar exam in Iowa and was pleased to be working in Richard Turner's office, in the back of my mind, I always thought I'd return home and set up a private practice.

But the phone had rung, and I'd found myself speaking with my grandmother again. I looked down at the floor and answered her, sensing by the tone of her voice that something was very wrong.

"Yassum."

"Tom, I have some bad news about that letter…"

I leaned on the kitchen counter and noticed the growing pile of dishes in the sink. I'd have to get to them soon, or we'd run out of room. Taking a deep breath, I looked back down at my feet and nodded.

"OK."

My grandmother shared that a man from the Tennessee Board of Law Examiners had shown up at her house that afternoon and asked her to return the letter they had sent just two weeks prior that had congratulated me on passing the multistate bar exam, which would have allowed me to practice law in Tennessee.

I was crestfallen. How could they take back something that I'd rightfully earned? When I inquired, my grandmother said she was not given a reason for the return of the letter. She said when the man asked her to return it, she stepped into the kitchen and promptly retrieved the letter from the drawer she had placed it in and walked back to the front door to hand over my right to practice law in the state of Tennessee.

I did not fault my grandmother for this. She did not make a practice of challenging white men. And even though the Jim Crow era had passed on paper, the rights of African Americans, particularly in the South, were far from equal. She knew the inherent dangers in questioning a white man in power and did what any reasonable person in her position would have done. Unfortunately, since that incident, which took place over forty years ago, there is still much work to be done if we are going to obtain true civil liberties for minorities in this country. This is evidenced by such inequities as the indiscriminate shootings of black men by police officers, the separation of minority children from their parents at the U.S. border, and the decades-long fight to abolish the suppression of minority votes in this country.

With one phone call, my Tennessee option was now closed. Even though I felt I was being discriminated against for being black and I could have sued the state of Tennessee, I decided to let the matter go when I'd first gotten the news since I already had a good job practicing law in the state of Iowa. After some time had passed and I'd thought better of it, I learned it was too late to sue, as the Tennessee Board of Law Examiners destroys their files after ten years.

After I got off the phone with my grandmother that night, I looked around my apartment. I'd done alright for myself. Sure, it was small. Just an efficiency, but it was just a few miles from work and the neighborhood was decent. Now that my brother Kenneth was living with me, I had a little extra spending money. In time, we'd be able to save up and find a bigger place. I sat down at the kitchen table and rubbed my forehead. Maybe this wasn't my battle to fight after all.

I thought back to the mid-1950s when my family and I lived on Johnny Lee's cotton farm in Haywood County,

Tennessee. I would have been about five at the time. We farmed about twenty acres for Mr. Lee. At that time, I was too young for farm work, but I enjoyed fetching water for my grandmother from the well and would often ask her if I could get her some more water. We drew our water from a deep well that had been dug into the ground. To get the water, you had to lower a bucket into the well with a rod in it. The rod would lift up to let in the water and drop back down to hold the water in the bucket.

One time, I jabbed a mule that wouldn't get out of my way when I was working the rod, and the mule kicked me square in the forehead. That kick knocked me out cold. I still have the scar and indentation in my forehead from that incident to remind me what happens when I don't choose my battles wisely. I learned right then and there not to antagonize stubborn asses, unless I was ready for a fight, a lesson that served me well when I learned about my home state revoking my right to practice law and even more so during my tenure in the Iowa state legislature.

A Cordial Environment

Determined to make the best of things, I worked as an assistant attorney general for the state of Iowa from 1974 to 1976. As an assistant attorney general, I was responsible for briefing and arguing criminal appeal cases before the Iowa Supreme Court and representing the Iowa Civil Rights Commission (ICRC) in discrimination cases. Even though this was my first job out of law school, I wasn't nervous. I had just taken and passed the Iowa Bar and was made to feel welcome by Turner's staff. I was pretty much in my element and fit right in.

Turner and I got along well. I, a Democrat, and he, a Republican. There was actually a pretty good mix of Democrats and Republicans working alongside each other. Unlike today's Congressional atmosphere and the atmosphere I have noticed in today's state legislatures, Democrats and Republicans worked well together back then. I had a good working relationship with the Criminal Appeals staff and would often go out and grab a beer with some of my coworkers after work.

My comrades at the office were Jim Robbins, Tom McGrane, David Dryer, David Lindquist, Nancy Shimanek, and Dottie Kelley. Robbins and McGrane were philosophically compatible. They were progressive Democrats like me. Dryer and Lindquist were Republicans. Shimanek was elected to the Iowa Senate as a Republican. Kelley was smart enough to keep her politics private. However, I always believed she was a Republican. And Dryer was a strong supporter of Richard Nixon. We, of course, gave him a hard time for supporting President Nixon, even when it was clear that Nixon was guilty of covering up the break-in into the Democratic National Committee's offices.

It was a pretty cordial working atmosphere with some good-natured teasing, and I gave as well as I got. When I shared how I was denied the multi-state bar license by the Tennessee Board of Law Examiners, my colleagues Jim Robbins, Dave Dryer, David Lindquist, Christy Fisher, and Tom McGrane all teased me about "failing" the exam and jokingly asserted that the state must have found out I was not of good moral character. It was their way of helping me cope with the fact that the state took back my acceptance letter.

Later on, I teased them when I obtained the right to practice law before the Eighth Circuit Court of Appeals, the District Court for the Southern and Northern Districts of Iowa, and the U. S. Supreme Court. I jokingly asserted that Robbins, Dryer, and others could not get admitted to practice before these bars because *they* were not of good moral character. As expected, they took it in stride, as was customary with these types of sardonic comments in our office.

When I first started working there, I did not have my own office. Instead, I shared an office and a phone with Ray Sullins, another assistant attorney general. This allowed him to assist and tutor me as I got up to speed on the casework. He tutored me for a few months while the rest of the offices were constructed. At the time, we were located in a converted house, and rooms were being built for me and my colleagues. Before that, Robbins, Dryer, and Lindquist sat around a table in the waiting area. They wrote and reviewed cases and wrote their briefs around that table. And sometimes I'd sit down and chat with them about their cases while they were working.

Even though we all had our own individual cases, we also worked well as a team. Once Attorney General Turner confiscated a small airplane from a defendant. The plane escheated to the state. Turner wanted to keep the plane for the attorney general's office and not turn it over to the state's travel pool. But he needed supporting law to keep the plane. I remember several of us leaving our offices and going over to the law library in the capitol to research this issue. Iowa has a beautiful state law library, and we spent hours in the stacks researching for him. All of us. I eventually found a case from Alaska that supported keeping the plane. It made Turner very happy. He ended up keeping the plane along with a 1973 Cadillac that was confiscated by the state using the same legal arguments.

We had a pretty decent view of the Capitol and the new Hoover Building, which was also under construction. Once the construction in our building was completed, we all moved into our new offices. They were small, but had the basics: a desk, a phone, and a few chairs for meetings. Christy Fisher was the office administrator. She worked closely with Ray Sullins. Christy, Debbie Cunningham, and Nancy Aisles typed our briefs and scheduled our arguments at the court. While not lawyers, they were as sharp as they come.

As an assistant attorney general, I worked under Ray's supervision. Initially, he assigned me single-issue cases until I became more familiar with criminal law. These were cases like guilty plea cases where the defendant pled to the charge. The guilty pleas ranged from simple misdemeanors to the spectrum of robberies, aggravated assaults, and other crimes. Later, I handled some major cases, such as the State vs. Pilcher (sodomy) and the State vs. Youngbear (murder). Our roles were not to try the cases. The county attorney prosecuted criminal violations at the county level. I worked at the state appellate level and worked to preserve a conviction when appealed to the appellate court from the county level.

As an assistant attorney general, I researched and wrote briefs that were filed with the Iowa Supreme Court. I also reviewed summaries of decisions from the high court. Once I began to be familiar with the case law, Ray assigned me some multiple-issue cases. The multiple-issue cases included any cases that raised more than one issue. It could be a couple of issues, or it could be as many as nine or ten. The defendant would have raised everything from improper pleadings to charges to lesser-included offenses, the court's evidentiary rulings, improper jury considerations, and improper convictions.

During the approximately two years that I worked there, I researched, briefed, and argued over fifty cases before the Iowa Supreme Court. And while I won more cases than I lost, I sometimes had cases that produced unintended results. On one occasion when arguing a case, Justice David Harris came down from the bench after closing arguments and said, "Mr. Mann, you're at your best when blowing your arguments."

Some of the cases I worked on were major cases, such as State v. Pilcher, State v. Youngbear, and In Re Oseing. State v. Pilcher was a case that challenged Iowa's sodomy laws. I had argued that the laws prohibiting sodomy in the state of Iowa should be upheld but was unsuccessful. Defendant Eugene Pilcher won the case, and the sodomy statute was struck down. While I did my best to brief and argue the case, secretly, I was pleased. My colleague Jim Robbins teased me and said there was nothing secret about it, as he could see my satisfaction with the outcome as clear as day when the Supreme Court's decision was rendered.

State v. Youngbear was a major case that presented the question of whether an Indian (Native American) who committed murder against another Indian while in Indian country (an Indian reservation) could be tried in the state courts. There were no prior decisions on this issue. This was a case of first impression and presented a new law. The Iowa Supreme Court held that both the state courts and the tribal courts had concurrent jurisdiction over Indians committing crimes in Indian country. This was a successful state appeal.

In Re Oseing was another case of first impression. The Iowa Supreme Court was asked to determine the due process rights of a person to be involuntarily held for a serious mental impairment. The court held that a person must be a danger to him or herself or others before they could be committed to a mental health facility for treatment. This first impression case changed Iowa's law. While I was not successful in my arguments in this case, I am pleased with the background work done in State v. Pilcher and In Re Oseing.

While working at the attorney general's office, I also met and worked with Roxanne Conlin, an assistant attorney general who is a well-known feminist and who had run for governor of Iowa. Roxanne represented the ICRC. I helped her represent the Commission in cases involving the district court. I observed her work and came to believe that she was the most skilled trial attorney I had ever met.

Bachelor Living

While I liked working at the attorney general's office, the pay was pretty low. We were only paid about $13,000 a year. Otherwise, I enjoyed making arguments before the Iowa Supreme Court and also appreciated the interoffice camaraderie. Initially, I lived alone in an efficiency apartment. A few months after I started working for the attorney general, my brother Kenneth came to live with me for a while. My uncle Al remained in Coralville and lived with my cousin Jesse. And my best friend Larry stayed in Iowa City.

I no longer had the 1968 Bonneville that I had purchased from my aunt and uncle when I was in Iowa City. Al and Larry and I had taken the Bonneville to Brownsville, Tennessee one time when we were visiting family. While we were there, Al took the car to visit some relatives and old acquaintances. The Bonneville was a convertible, and Al had let the top down. Unfortunately, it had rained and ruined the interior carpeting. My uncle hadn't learned how to put the top back up, and when he tried, he broke it. I didn't say anything to Al, as he was kind of sensitive, and I knew he didn't mean to break it. It was an old car, so I wasn't interested in spending money on trying to repair it. Instead, we traded the Bonneville in for a 1969 Dodge Super Bee. Larry and I purchased the car while we were living in Coralville. It was pretty fast and fun to drive.

I ended up trading the Super Bee in for a 1973 Pontiac Catalina before moving to Des Moines, though, because I was wanting a newer and more reliable car to get to and from work. Whenever I wanted to enjoy music in my apartment, I parked the car by my apartment window. I strung wires from the car through the apartment windows and attached the wires to an 8-Track player for entertainment. Since I only had one 8-Track player, I was constantly moving it between the car and the apartment. Aside from going out for beers with my coworkers, I had a pretty low-key social life. I met a young woman by the name of Cora

Douglas at a Christmas party for the governor's office. She was an aide to Governor Robert Ray and was working for a Republican like me, so we had that in common. We started dating soon after that party, and our relationship lasted for about six months. I liked staying close to home, so while we dated, we'd either spend time at my place or her apartment.

Everything changed, however, the day I met Leala Ann Salter. In the summer of 1975, Ray Sullins had hired a new law clerk to work in the attorney general's office. I was encouraged by the entire office to take Leala under my wing and to guide her in her work. I took this to mean that I should date her. Since she was quite cute and appeared to be very bright, I was extremely receptive to this idea. Fortunately, Leala was, too.

On our first date, we went out to a restaurant for dinner. Leala was quiet and shy. To a large extent, I was, too. While shy, Leala did have a confident way about her. She also did good legal research. I remember feeling instantly at ease with her and knew she was the woman I would one day marry. We dated exclusively for about a year. After a short courtship, she moved into the efficiency apartment with me.

Soon after, we got a bigger place, a two-bedroom apartment near Drake University, which was pretty close to work. We didn't have a lot of furnishing in the efficiency, so we purchased some additional items for our new place. I remember we'd enjoy lazy Sunday mornings together watching the CBS Sunday morning news. Leala has always been great company, and I was happy to discover that she was also a great cook. We'd go to the market and buy fresh meat and make lots of different dishes. We even discovered how to make jerky. My days of bachelor living and relying on Hamburger Helper were finally behind me.

Chapter 3

Beautiful Music

Alone we can do so little; together we can do so much.
— *Helen Keller*

Iowa Civil Rights Commission

I was admitted to practice law before the Eighth Circuit Court of Appeals on January 6th, 1976, just two years after being admitted to the Iowa Bar. Thomas McGrane from the Criminal Appeals Division made the motion to admit me to the Eighth Circuit. Then, almost seven months to the day of McGrane's motion, I was appointed by Governor Robert Ray to the position of executive director of the ICRC and served in that position for three years. As executive director, I was responsible for supervising a staff of thirty-one employees and was also in charge of budgeting, implementing civil rights statutes, advising on legislative proposals, and conducting public appearances while relating with external agencies and the press.

When I learned there was an opening for an executive director at the ICRC after former Executive Director Joseph Tate had been let go, I discussed applying for the position with my coworkers at the state attorney general's office. During my tenure with the state attorney general, I had worked on some cases with Roxanne Conlin who represented the ICRC, so I had some initial exposure to the commission and felt that would work in my favor.

My coworkers at the attorney general's office were very supportive of my interest in the position, so I decided to put my hat in the ring. Naturally, I reported back to them on the interviews I had with the gubernatorial-appointed interviewing committee and the governor. When they learned I had been appointed for the position by Governor Ray, they were happy for me and encouraged me to take the job. Because of the friendships I had made, I stayed in touch with many of my coworkers from the Criminal Appeals Division after I started working at the commission. I also had an assistant attorney general who was assigned to represent the ICRC since the nature of our work included some overlap, so it was easy to stay in touch.

A Hard Sell

One thing that wasn't easy, however, was convincing Leala to marry me. Leala and I had been dating for about a year and had been discussing the prospect of marriage for several months. When I started working for the ICRC, I decided it was time to settle down. I went out and picked out a simple gold engagement ring my first week on the job. And when I got home from work that evening, I got down on one knee and proposed to Leala.

Unfortunately, she didn't jump at the chance to marry me, and it wasn't because she didn't like the ring I picked out. "You're just wanting this because of your appointment to the ICRC," she stated. I assured her that wasn't the case, offering her the ring in my extended hand. But Leala shook her head. "It's a high-profile position that will bring public exposure. Are you sure this isn't why you want to get married now?"

I stood up and looked her square in the eyes and said, "I promise on all that I have and all that is to come that the only reason I am asking you to marry me is because I love you, and

I want to spend the rest of my life with you." Leala's eyes teared up and she reached over and hugged me, sobbing. Fortunately, this was all it took, and Leala said yes as I helped her place the engagement ring on her finger.

Once Leala had accepted my proposal, I asked Chief Justice C. Edwin Moore of the Iowa Supreme Court if we could use the Supreme Court's chambers for the marriage ceremony, and if he would perform the ceremony. He agreed to both requests and made the majestic walls of his courtroom in the Des Moines Capitol available to us. It was a magnificent gesture by a very good man.

Leala and I were married on July 24th, 1976, with Chief Moore presiding. Uncle Alfred stood with me as the best man. And the whole gang from the Criminal Appeals Division of the attorney general's office was also there wishing us well. Leala wore a beautiful blue and white dress, and I wore a dark three-piece suit with a gray tie. The only hitch that occurred was when I made a last-minute decision to replace Jim Robbins as best man with Alfred when my uncle unexpectedly showed up with my cousin Jesse. Jim agreed to step aside without any rancor and hosted our wedding reception at his lovely home in Des Moines.

The Robbins' Beaverdale home was a nice, white, brick home with three or four bedrooms. Our coworkers and friends from the attorney general's office attended the reception, and Al Maclin and Jesse Currie from my family were also there. It was a festive atmosphere. I remember there was a nice spread for us to enjoy, and Jim's wife Linda had baked and served a beautiful wedding cake for us. We also spent some time at the end opening our gifts.

Leala and I did not take an immediate honeymoon. Instead, we drove 4,000 miles down to Mexico City during the summer of 1978. We visited the Floating Gardens at Mexico City and the pyramids north of Mexico City. On our way down, we drove through the Sierra Madre Mountains. The roads were narrow, and the mountains were steep and frightening, so we found a different way to drive back.

Our First Home

Soon after we were married, Leala and I decided to buy a house. We hired a realtor from Iowa Realty to guide us in our housing search. A few weeks in, however, we thought we were going to have to terminate her services because she kept steering us to dilapidated houses in ghetto areas. Rather than making a big fuss of it, we simply rejected the proffers outright and were about to dismiss her when she finally got the message and began to take us to more desirable neighborhoods. I think it was the frowns on our faces and the outright rejections that let her know we were not interested in the houses we were being offered.

One of the homes she showed us was a three-bedroom brick home with a large basement and a bar in a nice middle-class neighborhood out on Lower Beaver Road. It had a master bedroom and two additional bedrooms on the upper floor. There was one bath on the upper floor and a furnished basement with a wet bar. Both levels were carpeted. And in addition to the large family room in the basement, there was a room for my pool table and a laundry room. We immediately fell in love with the property and decided to put an offer on it right away.

After closing on the sale, we moved into our new home. After my appointment to ICRC, there was press coverage. Soon after, however, I began to receive telephone calls at our home number from anonymous persons threatening my life. I was called racial names, including the "N" word, and subjected to unwanted and threatening comments, including being told to return to Africa. I reported this to Dan Johnston, County Attorney for Polk County, Iowa. There wasn't much that he could offer as help, other than tapping my telephone and listening to all the conversations. So, I began to retaliate. A call would come in threatening me, and I would return the favor, hurling insults back at them. It went on like this until they eventually tired of calling me.

Family began to arrive soon after we moved into our home. They came intermittently. Fortunately, we had that big basement, which afforded them some privacy during their visits.

I don't remember the order, but I know that Jesse Currie, Kenneth Maclin, and Robert Maclin came and stayed with us for a while. As did Leala's brother George Salter, his wife, and their two kids. We helped them find an apartment soon after, but they ended up moving back to Texas after living in Iowa for a year or so, claiming the winters were too bitter. Fred Maclin (uncle Buddy's grandson), Floyd Maclin, Jr., Floyd LaFragia Maclin's son, and my younger brothers Keith Maclin and Derek L. Maclin also stayed with us. And later, I moved my mom and my sisters Yvonne and Michelle to Des Moines. My mom lived with us until Leala and I found her an apartment close by. My extended family came to visit later.

The Bolero

When I started at the Commission, the governor's assistant, Wythe Willey, took me to meet my new staff. Wythe introduced me as the new director, and I told them to be at ease so they would know I was not there to clean house and fire everybody. Instead, I started my work at the Commission by inviting, one-by-one, each of the approximately thirty-one staff members to meet with me in my cubicle. I asked each staffer to tell me what their job was at the Commission and to say what they thought my job was. I learned a lot about the commission during my first three or four weeks when I met with my staff and listened to them as they shared their impressions with me.

The Bolero, a documentary by Alan Miller and William Fertik that had received an Academy Award, had come out in

1973, and I discovered it when watching PBS one evening. I was impressed with the way the musicians joined in and worked together to achieve the music. In my first few months in office I was looking for ways to make the staff cohesive in light of the fact that there had been some discord between the previous director and the commission.

I asked Michael Bailey, my compliance director, to see if he could find a copy of the film. He was able to find a copy at the state library, which we were able to show to our staff. I had the staff assemble in the large conference room to hear my vision of how we would operate before I presented the film.

We watched as Zubin Mehta and the Los Angeles Philharmonic Orchestra prepared and then played the "Bolero." We listened as they first explained what they were going to do and then did it. We watched as the musicians warmed up, tuned up, rehearsed, and then played in perfect harmony. From the drums, to the flutist, to the horns and the bassoonist, it was beautiful. Everyone was working in harmony. They played until the music ended in a crescendo. This film won an award for the Best Documentary at the 46th Academy Awards and can now be seen on YouTube.

After watching the film, I explained to my staff that my vision was that we would work together in harmony, like the musicians in the film. The intake personnel would receive and document complaints of discrimination. The clerical staff would process the complaints. The investigators would investigate and determine whether discrimination had occurred or not. The supervisors would direct the activities of the investigators and assist them in completing their duties timely. Together, we would tackle and eliminate the large backlog of cases that had accumulated at the Commission. We'd keep it simple: We'd all work in harmony as part of a team. To me, that was the way to go.

Everyone was attentive during the performance. I asked Bailey to check with my staff to see if they had enjoyed the film afterward, and I received a positive report. It was my intent to build a workforce that would work seamlessly together just like the musicians in the film. So, there I was. About ten years out of the cotton fields. Conducting. Cajoling. Encouraging. And directing. I was the new executive director for the ICRC, and I was doing my job. I was leading my staff. This was beautiful music.

Chapter 4

Flip-Jank

"Well," I said, "I reckin I learned not to trade with Christians."
— Forrest Carter, The Education of Little Tree

New Relationships

Throughout my tenure at the ICRC, I worked to create new relationships, first with my staff and eventually with the commissioners, starting with Chair Gretchen Lee and later with her successor, Gretchen Bataille. Commissioners were unsure of me, since they had not hired me. So, I worked to assuage their concerns, recognizing that commissioners were appointed to the Commission to represent particular political interest groups.

The Commission was made up of a pretty diverse group on the Commission. There was Charles Toney, a strong African American commissioner from Davenport. He represented employers, the entities that most of the civil rights claims were filed against. There was George Garcia, a Native American who represented the Native Americans in the state. And there were women, such as Evelyne Villines, who represented the disabled, and Rachel Evans, who became chair after Bataille left. Evans was a supporter of mine and represented employers. We had a good working relationship. I had to walk a fine line between the commissioners and the governor. It wasn't always easy, but for the most part I learned how to appease both.

The commissioners could not terminate my services. Only the governor could. They could have input, but that was it. The commissioners were also appointed by the governor. Traditionally, the commissioners' role had been to hire the director and manage all of the staff up to the director. Under the new paradigm, however, that had changed. Commissioners could tell me how to manage my staff, but I wasn't obligated to follow directives. I had an additional boss, the governor, to look to for direction. By accommodation, it was agreed that the commissioners could set general policy, and I would follow that policy. For example, they could tell me to take a certain action and then I could decide how to accomplish that action and what route to take.

During my tenure at the ICRC, I remember philosophical discussions that I had with Commissioner Charles Toney of Davenport, Iowa, about the Ku Klux Klan (KKK). Commissioner Toney and I discussed the KKK at length. I remember he rejected the idea that the KKK should be free to march and express their ideas. Whereas, while I didn't support their agenda, I supported their constitutional right to free expression and marching. Our discussions never became heated, but they were serious conversations. Commissioner Toney and I would talk about the proverbial act of yelling "fire" in a movie theater. Neither of us supported that. But I did support nonviolent free speech. We talked about Skokie, Illinois, where the Nazis and the KKK marched. I was for it, whereas Toney did not feel the Nazis and the KKK should be allowed to march because of their hate-filled agendas.

While at the ICRC, I learned that I had to sharpen my public game. Shortly after my appointment, I was invited by the Director of the Department of Social Services to meet with him and his staff and to make some comments about affirmative action. "Affirmative action" is any positive action that contributes toward the greater utilization of minorities, women, the elderly, and the disabled, including goals established by units and timetables for completion. The ultimate purpose of affirmative action is to provide equal opportunity for all persons to prevent the continuation of discriminatory practices and to redress patterns of minority and female underutilization.

I went to this meeting, but unfortunately, I was unprepared. During the meeting I could not properly answer all of the questions posed to me by a well-prepared social services staff. It was embarrassing. I went before a group of affirmative action coordinators and did not know the subject matter. It was a lesson that I never forgot. After that meeting, I learned all of the affirmative action issues and prepared well for any future meetings. I did this by studying the civil rights statute from beginning to end and becoming well-versed on it. I did not rely on any staff for this work. I learned the subject matter and made my own presentations. And I retained each written presentation so that I could improve upon it at the next presentation.

Trouble in Paradise

Part of my job was to hire field staff and manage that staff. I had to ensure that the staff conducted timely, quality investigations of complaints. The quality and quantity of investigations were essential. And the development and promotion of staff was important to that end. Its peripheral impact on public education, prevention, and affirmative action was pivotal.

On November 4th, 1977, Arthur Bonfield stated the ICRC had made great strides since I was named director. Bonfield had been my Constitutional Law professor at the University of Iowa, and he was an expert on constitutional issues. He felt that changing the lines of authority would make the commission operate even better. He said that doing away with the commissioners and having the governor appoint a head of the commission would streamline matters. I was ambivalent about the legislative action that allowed the governor to appoint the director. After all, the governor appointed me. However, I felt that it would lead to a natural conflict between two bosses. Fortunately, I was able to co-opt commissioners as soon as they were appointed. The governor's office had little active involvement in commission activities that I recall, and I avoided conflict, for the most part, by working with the commissioners directly.

Chairwoman Gretchen Bataille said Bonfield's plan was well thought out. However, she feared it would give a considerable amount of political power to the governor's office. Governor Ray supported civil rights, but the next governor might not, so the proposed changes might not be in the best interest of minorities and those discriminated against in the state of Iowa. She also stated that publicizing the complaints could cause problems for the claimants in the workplace, which could affect them not just in the current job but also in their ability to find work elsewhere, after being branded as a troublemaker.

Chair Bataille was correct in that changing the procedures to publicize the complaints could have a negative impact on complainants. It is a very difficult proposition to file a complaint. A current employer can and often does retaliate. Retaliation could be enhanced if another potential employer knew of the filing of a complaint and then participated in the blackballing of the complainant. Lifting the publicity on complaints could educate the public about discrimination issues; however, it could also discourage victims of discrimination from filing a complaint. This issue was resolved by the legislature by maintaining the privacy of complaints. The question of educating the public was addressed by publishing case reports that had gone through litigation. It was my idea to publish these reports, which identified the complainants as well as the respondents. I drafted the first volume of these case reports and worked well with Chair Bataille and all the other commissioners until Al Parrish and Annette Pieper were appointed.

Council Bluffs Housing Study

Because of confidentiality laws applicable to civil rights cases, we were limited to the amount of information that could be disclosed to the public about specific cases. To bypass this obstacle, and to achieve our intended educational impact, we resorted to the technique of the special study, or investigational exposé. One such exposé resulted in ICRC's publication "Don't Tell the Civil Rights People," a study of discriminatory sales and rental practices toward blacks in the housing market in Council Bluffs, Iowa.

For this study, we tracked the availability of rental housing and uncovered a coding system that was designed to deny available units to blacks. We discovered that rental applications were coded in the following manner: the words "nice people" written on a rental application meant no blacks; the words "good people" meant no hippie types; and the drawing of a smiling face meant no blacks. This study was organized by ICRC's Education Director, Terry Dolphin. Kudos should also go to ICRC's Commissioner Jack Peters of Council Bluffs for supporting this study of his home community. Follow-up studies revealed that this exposé had the initial impact of altering discriminatory practices across the state, particularly in Council Bluffs. The studies were not done in perpetuity, however, so this did not resolve all problems of housing discrimination.

Six-Player Basketball

During my tenure, I urged the commissioners to improve and expand the ICRC's interpretative rules and regulations. In one case, we addressed the controversial area of discrimination in disabilities and athletics. We observed that, in Iowa, high school girls were still playing six-player basketball. In six-player basketball, there were three defensive players and three offensive players. The defensive players did not cross the center of the court. Instead, the ball was moved to the center of the court by the defense and passed over to the offense. The offense only played offense and the defense only played defense. Thus, the players only developed their defensive or offensive skills. By 1979, college female basketball teams had moved to the five-player game where the team played the whole court, both defense and offense. Consequently, girls playing six-player basketball were at a disadvantage for earning college scholarships as they were not skilled in both offensive and defensive playing.

Unfortunately, the six-player basketball tradition for girls was strong in Iowa. Wayne Cooley, Executive Secretary of the Iowa Athletic Union, and Governor Robert Ray had opposed the change to five-player basketball. So, I proposed a rule that would have doomed six-player basketball and require that Iowa's colleges shift large sums of money from men to women's athletic scholarships. The commissioners voted 6-1 to adopt the new rule. Governor Ray threatened a veto. However, we pushed it through, knowing it would get killed on the governor's desk. As a result of our defiance, Commissioners Gretchen Bataille and Eugene Williams were not reappointed to the Commission by Governor Ray. While the Iowa legislature objected to the Commission's rule, the end of six-player basketball was in sight.

Linda Eaton

In January of 1979, Linda Eaton, the only female firefighter with the Iowa City Fire Department, sought to breastfeed her four-month old baby while at work. The Fire Department, however, sought to punish Ms. Eaton by threatening to fire her. In turn, she pursued a complaint with the Iowa City Human Rights Commission (ICRC) and then filed with the Johnson County District Court. I had Michael Bailey notify Ms. Eaton's attorneys that the ICRC would pursue an expeditious resolution of any claim filed with the ICRC. She then filed with the ICRC, and the district court delayed any action that the court would take until the ICRC had completed its work.

Ms. Eaton asserted discrimination. Iowa law required a complainant to exhaust all administrative remedies before pursuing a claim in court. Exhaustion of administrative remedies meant that Ms. Eaton had to file a claim with the ICRC. A local judge, Ansel J. Chapman, issued an injunctive ruling allowing Ms. Eaton to feed her baby pending a ruling by the ICRC. In March of 1979, the ICRC issued a ruling that there was probable cause to believe that Ms. Eaton had been discriminated against because of her sex. The case was conciliated, and Ms. Eaton was finally permitted to breastfeed her baby at work.

Disability Cases

Through chosen representatives, the people of Iowa established a public policy of non-discrimination, including prohibiting discrimination because of disability in employment. Additionally, federal law contained in The Rehabilitation Act of 1973, prohibits discrimination on the basis of disability. In both cases, the law prohibits an employer from discriminating in employing or in promoting any person on account of a physical or mental disability that is unrelated to the person's qualifications and ability to perform a job. Both require that an employer reasonably accommodate the known physical or mental disabilities of an applicant for employment or a present employee.

The ICRC drafted a rule to clarify the requirement that employers reasonably accommodate the disabled. Consistent with the federal requirements, the Iowa redraft required an employer to reasonably accommodate the disabled by supplying a reader if the disabled person was blind and the job included paperwork; supplying an interpreter if the disabled person was deaf and the job required telephone contact; supplying adequate workspace and access to it if the disabled person used a wheelchair; and allowing for minor adjustments in working hours if the disabled person was required to visit a clinic or rehabilitation center for treatment during the work day.

Obviously, the reasonable accommodation requirements demanded changes and adjustments in what was once considered to be normal, daily routines. Like other civil rights laws, the disability discrimination laws were another manifestation of a massive national drive to right wrongs prevailing in our social and economic structures.

On July 14th, 1978, the ICRC took on a disability discrimination and retaliation case. Farnum v. Hoerner Waldorf Company was a prima facie case of unlawful employment discrimination established when the complainant, Hazel Farnum, showed that she had injured herself on the job while lifting heavy bags. However, in spite of her disability, she could still perform the basic employment tasks of lifting items that were under twenty pounds. She could not, however, perform a non-basic employment task (lifting heavier items) because of her disability, and she was subsequently terminated for failure to perform the non-basic employment task that was prohibited by her doctor. On April 26th, 1976, a deputy industrial commissioner had determined that Ms. Farnum had sustained a ten percent permanent partial industrial disability.

Ms. Farnum was successful in her disability discrimination claim and was awarded back wages.

Backlog of Cases

Like most human rights agencies, the ICRC placed a great emphasis upon an expeditious resolution of a complaint. The ICRC had a large case inventory—over nine hundred complaints—and many of those had been on ICRC's docket prior to my arrival. Complainants and respondents alike justifiably cried out for quicker resolutions of these cases.

I tried to respond. In August of 1976, with the support and aid of Governor Robert Ray, the ICRC entered into a cooperative effort with ACTION. As a result, the ICRC received assistance from VISTA, Volunteers in Service to America. VISTA lent volunteers to the ICRC, and they worked as investigators. This project spanned twenty-two months. While we had some success, it was relatively small. The major defect in the program was that VISTA volunteers were only available to ICRC for about a year. Given the time needed to train the volunteers, we were not able to get maximum effectiveness out of the VISTA program. Nevertheless, during these twenty-two months, we were able to close 542 cases with the help of regular staff and VISTA volunteers, which was over half of the backlog.

In August of 1979, I was nominated by the Democratic Party to run for the state senate seat being vacated by Earl Willits. At a commission meeting on August 10th, 1979, Al Parrish and Annette Pieper raised issues about the commission's case inventory. Parrish asserted that this was a serious problem, with "the little people out there" wanting procedures for faster case resolutions.

While I agreed that we needed to address the backlog of cases, the commissioners seemed to place blame on me and the Commission for the backlog and wanted state laws simplified to speed up the handling of the cases. I explained to them that it wasn't the complexity of the laws that was causing the backlog, but rather the fact that the Commission was underfunded and short-staffed. I let them know that if they had a problem with my performance that they should just fire me. Parrish denied ulterior motives and stated that he wanted to explore alternative solutions to the backlog problem.

Everybody wanted faster resolutions. The governor wanted faster resolutions, the commissioners wanted faster resolutions, and I wanted faster resolutions. But I was not in agreement with Parrish's proposal for "rapid charge processing" that would have essentially substituted a form or weak mediation for strong investigative enforcement. I wasn't willing to quickly and easily throw away charging parties' rights to a due process investigation. And I said so.

When Parrish made his assertion about the backlog problem, I immediately suspected the involvement of the governor and a political motive. I stated that I resented the implications by Parrish and Pieper that the Commission had done nothing to address the problem and said, "If the Commission feels that I'm not properly executing my job, that's what you ought to say. Your obvious step is to say to the governor that we need a new director."

Parrish countered and said that he wasn't questioning anybody's ability to do the job but only "whether we can come up with solutions with some alternatives to the problem." I disagreed with him and added, "It seems to me that you've got a second agenda that you're not exposing to the commission." Parrish just stared back at me and failed to respond.

Parrish, like Governor Ray, was a Republican. I was of the view that the new procedures he was proposing would not solve the case inventory and said, "The best alternative is for the legislature to live up to its commitment and make the agency stable, with sufficient budgetary support. If we had been properly funded in the first place, the backlog would never have developed."

My immediate suspicion of ulterior motives during this Commission meeting reminded me of a time when my Uncle Alfred and Cousin Ruth and I were playing with persimmons on Johnny Lee's farm in Tennessee. We played mostly made-up games when we were kids because we usually did not have store-bought toys. Whenever we played "'simmons", Alfred, Ruth, and I would often go into the fields and pastures and pick persimmons from the trees. We'd place the ripe fruit on the end of a stick and flip them at each other or some other target.

In one incident, Alfred accidentally flipped a persimmon at Ruth and hit her under her right eye. Ruth started bawling. Nonstop. My uncle tried to console her, but she pushed him away and grabbed a persimmon and placed it on a stick and aimed it right at Al. "I'm going to hit you with a 'simmon," she declared a few times between sobs. To mollify her and prevent a counterattack, Alfred told her that it was just a "flip-jank" and then shot me a knowing look. This made-up word sounded important to my young cousin, and it seemed to mean that things were OK because she eventually stopped crying and threatening to hit Al with a 'simmon, so we continued playing until it was time to head home for supper.

While the incident with the persimmons was just an accident, my uncle had stretched the truth a bit by making up a word to appease my cousin and to bring quick resolution to the incident. And when the Commission was coming down on me for the backlog in cases at the ICRC, it made me think of this incident, and I started to wonder if they were trying to pull a flip-jank on me by not revealing the real reason for their concern over the backlog of cases, which is why I reacted so strongly.

Civil Rights

I have always been a strong advocate for civil rights. While at the ICRC, I received little or no direction from the governor. Most of my contact was with Susan Mickelson, the governor's administrative assistant. So, I set my own course. After taking on such hotly debated issues as housing discrimination and six-player girls' basketball, I began to suspect that the governor was not in accord with my thinking. My supporters Gretchen Bataille and Rev. Eugene Williams had not been reappointed. Both had supported rules proposed by me to declare six-player girls' basketball discriminatory. Bataille was told by the governor's staff that the decision to not reappoint her was made after the basketball rules were adopted. The governor would appoint new commissioners, and I would co-opt them. I worked to assuage their concerns, recognizing that commissioners were appointed to the Commission to represent particular political interest groups.

The Civil Rights Act of 1964 and the Voting Rights Act of 1965 were important pieces of legislation moving in the direction of providing an opportunity for a free and equitable life for all black people. While working for the ICRC, I made speeches to encourage young black voters to exercise their voting rights at the polls.

In a speech that I gave to the Black American Law Students Association in February of 1978, I reminded them, "Although many legal impediments to the right to vote have been removed, in some states substantial numbers of black voters are still prevented from exercising their right to vote because of irregularities, which include late opening of polling places, inoperative voting machines, and incorrect delivery of voting machines to predominantly black precincts."

I reminded these students of the importance of exercising their civil rights to vote that others had fought for them to obtain, adding, "While there has been progress in overcoming legal impediments to the right to vote, there still remains a failure by blacks to participate in the political process in sufficient numbers to bring about much-needed political changes."

In hopes of increasing voter turnout, I shared that "it gains us nothing to secure a legal right to vote and then to fail to exercise that right…and then to fail to identify and support qualified minority and female candidates." As I reflect on these words from my speech given over forty years ago, the words could not be more timely today.

On September 24th, 1965, President Lyndon Johnson issued an executive order requiring government contractors to take "affirmative action" to hire without regards to race, creed, color or national origin. In addition to having legally prohibited discrimination in employment, President Johnson was requiring companies that contracted with the government to take "affirmative action" to hire minorities.

It was not only important for me to know and understand the meaning of affirmative action and its legal requirements, but also to know the moral rationale for the requirement. From a historical perspective, blacks were introduced to this nation as slaves. The American Revolution was fought over the right of self-governance, equality, liberty, and the pursuit of happiness. It turns out, America's most important credal statement was both racist and sexist. In the first draft of the Declaration of Independence, Thomas Jefferson accused King George of "waging a cruel war against human nature" by "captivating and carrying them (blacks) into slavery in another hemisphere." Unfortunately, this language was opposed by southern states that had built their economies on slave labor. As a result, the final draft of the Declaration of Independence declared all men to be created equal without addressing the question of slavery.

Even before the Declaration of Independence, America could not bring itself to treat all of its citizens equally. In 1771, the Articles of Confederation, predecessor to the United States Constitution, were adopted. American slaves were to be counted for voting purposes. Representation in Congress was to be based on the population within a state. Slaves were to be counted as property and as three-fifths of a person for taxation and representation. The United States Constitution was adopted in 1787. However, because it made no mention of slavery, it was essentially permitting slavery.

Article II of the Constitution stated that any person who was not a citizen could not vote. At the time, slaves were considered property, not citizens. This was affirmed when the United States Supreme Court ruled in 1856 in the Dred Scott Decision that "a black man had no rights which a white man was required to respect." Fortunately, I learned that Iowa had a better history. Before it became a state, the territorial Supreme Court of Iowa ruled in "the Matter of Ralph" that Ralph, a slave sent to Iowa to earn money working in the lead mines of Dubuque, and whose owner had sought to reclaim him in 1839, was declared a free man.

In 1863, President Abraham Lincoln freed the slaves in the Emancipation Proclamation. In 1865, a 13th Amendment to the United States Constitution abolished slavery. In 1866, the 14th Amendment to the United States Constitution guaranteed all citizens due process and equal protection of the laws. The 15th Amendment guaranteed the right to vote for blacks in 1869, and the 19th Amendment guaranteed the right to vote for women in 1919. The Civil Rights Act of 1866, prohibited denial of constitutional rights under color of state law. And the Civil Rights Act of 1871 prohibited discrimination in employment and guaranteed the right to contract on the basis of race.

While all these legal changes and affirmative conduct had taken place, there was objection when it became known that "affirmative action" in government employment was being required. In 1979 in United Steelworkers of America, AFL-CIO-CLC v. Weber, the United States Supreme Court held that Title VII of the Civil Rights Act of 1964 did not prohibit race-conscious affirmative action plans. This ruling was important to creating an atmosphere in the country where voluntary compliance with civil rights laws could prevail.

I knew, as most civil rights workers knew, and as President Johnson probably knew, that while laws cannot change beliefs, they can change conduct, which is why President Johnson issued his Executive Order calling for affirmative action. While we have made progress with civil rights in this country, there is much still to accomplish. As one anonymous southern preacher said, "Lord, we ain't what we ought to be. We ain't what we want to be. We ain't where we are going to be. But thank the Lord, we ain't what we was."

In-House Training

As executive director, part of my job was to hire field staff and manage that staff. So, I set about the business of training the commissioners, supervisors, investigators, and intake staff to recognize and take good complaints so they could conduct thorough investigations. It wouldn't do any good to have a good claim taken by the intake staff if the investigators did not recognize it as a good claim. It also wouldn't do any good to have a good investigation if the supervisors rejected the investigation. Nor would it be beneficial to process a complaint through good intake, through a quality investigation, through supervisory review, only to have the commissioners reject it. So, everyone, including the director, had to be in continuous training.

In view of this, the management staff and I started in-house training. I received support from several colleagues appointed by the governor during our efforts to educate our staff. Sue Follon, director of the Iowa Commission on the Status of Women, was supportive. Colleen Shearer, director of Job Service of Iowa, was also supportive. And Ms. Shearer joined me in bringing Rev. C.T. Vivian, a Dr. Martin Luther King lieutenant, to Des Moines to do race-conscious sensitivity training.

Soon after, I formed a coalition with the executive directors within the Equal Employment Opportunity Commission's (EEOC's) Region VII to conduct this training. The ICRC had jurisdiction over claims of discrimination in employment, public accommodations, and housing. Most of the cases were employment related. The commission was a deferral agency of the federal EEOC, which meant employment cases were also within the jurisdiction of the EEOC. It made more sense for the EEOC to defer cases in Iowa to the ICRC for processing than for there to be simultaneous processing of the same claims. The same was true for Nebraska, Missouri, and Kansas, states within the EEOC's Region VII.

So, at the suggestion of Lawrence Myers, the executive director of the Nebraska Equal Opportunity Commission, the Region VII Executive Council on Civil Rights (RECCR) was formed to spearhead the training. We provided seminars to commissioners and staff of both state and local human rights commissions throughout the region.

The training started with a jurisdictional review of whether the complaint named a proper complainant and respondent, whether the complaint was timely within the EEOC's and human rights agency's statute of limitations, and whether there was evidentiary support for the complaint.

Employment discrimination complaints are generally disparate treatment complaints, and reviews seek to determine whether the complainant has been treated differently from non-protected classes or employees. We taught that complaints had to be proven by a standard of "reasonable cause" or "probable cause" to believe that discrimination had occurred. The quantity of evidence required of a party having the burden of proof is a preponderance of the evidence. Accordingly, reasonable cause exists when there are reasonable grounds of suspicion supported by facts and circumstances strong enough in themselves to warrant a cautious person to believe that discrimination had occurred.

We taught our commissioners and staff that evidence consists of the testimony of the witnesses and all the material facts and circumstances proven in the case. To establish a prima facie case of disparate treatment discrimination, a claimant had to show that s(he) belonged to a protected class group, that s(he) was treated differently than similarly situated persons, and that the differential treatment was because of the claimant's minority status.

While proof of discriminatory intent is required in a disparate treatment case, direct proof of intent is not necessary. Intent can be shown in some situations by merely showing the differences in treatment. Proof of discrimination does not ordinarily come by way of confession, but rather discriminatory motivation and intent often can only be proved through circumstantial evidence. A plaintiff is not required to prove that protected class status (i.e., age, sex, or race) was the defendant's sole or exclusive consideration but must prove that protected class status was "a determinative factor" in the employer's decision.

We taught that a prima facie case of sexual harassment can be proven when an employee shows that a plaintiff is a member of a protected class; that a plaintiff was subjected to unwelcome verbal or physical conduct of a sexual nature; that, but for her sex, a plaintiff would not have been subjected to the sexual conduct; that the sexual conduct was sufficiently severe or pervasive that it unreasonably interfered with plaintiff's work performance, or it created an intimidating, hostile, or offensive working environment; and that the defendant knew, or should have known, of the harassment but failed to take immediate and appropriate corrective action.

We also taught that human rights agencies were established by legislatures as an integral part of the social revolution of the 1960s. We shared that agencies were established because there had been a lack of meaningful access to the courts by civil rights complainants because of their lack of financial resources or obstacles to their hiring a lawyer because of their race or sex. In many situations, black Americans could not get lawyers to take their cases because of the negative social stigma surrounding the representation of race cases. The lawyers who took on these cases would, in turn, become pariahs in their own communities. Human rights agencies were developed as an alternative to the courts. Agencies would be allowed to develop expertise, determine the existence of a problem, and provide a remedy. They would both investigate claims and issue determinations.

We, therefore, taught our commissioners and staff that the burden was on them to do quality work. They learned that they needed to work quickly and efficiently. They also had to develop the necessary expertise and to be able to make and issue decisions on a consistent basis. Agencies had to learn to educate the public on their actions and the reasons for taking these actions. There was a greater demand for accountability and improved efficiency. We also were working to eliminate large case inventories, and we felt that training would help all parties achieve this goal.

Educating the Public

As H. G. Wells once said, "The difference between catastrophe and history is education." Early on, I made the decision to take the Commission on the road so we could educate the public on the work we were doing. I persuaded the commissioners to hold their monthly meetings in different cities across the state of Iowa. While this was taking place, there was local and statewide media coverage of the training. We would let the light in, to the extent that we could with statutory enforced privacy over individual cases, and the public would know what the Commission was doing. It was our way of educating the public on civil rights issues and gaining public support for the Commission.

There are local human rights commissions in many cities across the state of Iowa. Local commissions were invited to host the state commission and to advise of the prevalent issues in their communities. At these settings, the commissioners and I could urge upon the local city councils that the state commission was not the answer to all the problems of discrimination prevalent in the Iowa economy. We asserted that there also was a continuing and growing need for an effective enforcement agency at the local level, and we would give our support to the local agency in this symbiotic relationship.

I had also sought and received support from the wider civil rights community. Larry Carter, president of the Des Moines Branch NAACP, gave strong support, as did Mary Robinson, president of the Iowa-Nebraska State Conference of the NAACP. I was invited to and spoke to several Iowa branches of the NAACP, including Fort Dodge, Marshalltown, and Cedar Rapids.

At Cedar Rapids, I addressed the aims of the NAACP, which are to eliminate racial discrimination and segregation from all aspects of life in America, to secure a free ballot for every qualified American citizen, to seek justice in the courts, to secure legislation banning discrimination and segregation, and to end mob violence and police brutality. Unfortunately, none of these problems had been resolved on November 18th, 1977, when I spoke at Cedar Rapids, and they have not been resolved today.

In addition to speaking to the public, we produced an annual report of the Commission's activities that was made available to public officials and libraries. Terry Dolphin, the Commission's Education Director, drafted this brochure in 1977. We also started and produced a compilation of case decisions issued by the Commission. These were included in a series of case reports that were released from 1965 to 1979.

In a speech that I gave to the Community Career Center for Women, the Small Business Administration, and the Small Business Committee at the Greater Des Moines Chamber of Commerce in February of 1979, I emphasized the importance of educating others on affirmative action so we could address discrimination on a broader scale. In my speech, I shared that "sometimes I believe that our struggle is difficult, not because our struggle is unjust, for justice is on our side, but rather because we have failed to convince all Iowans that the motto of the state does not simply impose a standard of performance upon our agency, but imposes itself upon all citizens. For it is we, the collective people of the state, who prize our liberties, and it is we who will maintain our rights. ... As former Vice President Nelson Rockefeller put it, 'The nourishing of the American system requires a sense of responsibility, not only on the part of individual citizens, but ... on the part of America's leadership. ... To the extent that they do not exercise their power and influence in the direction of the common good, they are undermining the very system that has given them that power and influence.'" Over thirty-nine years ago, I concluded my speech, encouraging those in attendance to prize their civil liberties and to take an active role in preserving them. Given today's political climate, it would behoove us to do the same.

Chapter 5

A Vacant Seat

There is no telling how many miles you will have to run while chasing a dream.

— Author Unknown

George Blake

When I was a young boy, we lived in Browns Creek, Tennessee. During that time, we didn't have access to public transportation, so my siblings, cousins, uncle, and I walked about two miles each day to school. Rain or shine. Browns Creek Elementary School was small and unassuming: It only had two rooms and two teachers. Looking back, there wasn't much that stood out about this school per se, but I do have one event that is forever etched into my memory. It was the day I got into my first real fight.

I don't know what specifically caused the fight, except that we Maclins were a poor but proud family. We carried ourselves as such and wore our pride on our shirt sleeves. Some folks resented this, as they perceived our pride as attitude, which must have threatened them on some level. On the day of the fight, my classmate George Drake and his supporters approached me. I had my Uncle Al and my other family members with me. Since it was a small school, there were two camps: The Maclins and everybody else. We Maclins were taught to never start fights. However, we stood up for ourselves whenever provoked.

On this particular day, I remember we were all having lunch, and George Drake started to pick a fight with me. I responded in kind and pretty soon, I realized I could not whip him, so I bit into his forearm and refused to let go until the principal came and pulled me off of him. George was yelping and twisting, trying to get away, but I wasn't going to lose face in front of the others and kept a good hold on him until the principal arrived. Ever since that day, I learned what I was made of and that if I wanted something badly enough, I just needed to hold on and ride out the storm. Not one to carry grudges, I decided to put the event with my classmate behind me. Fortunately, George did the same, and we were able to finish out our schooling together without further incident.

Special Election

On July 31st, 1979, I learned that my state senator and fellow democrat, Earl Willits, had resigned from the Iowa General Assembly and was leaving his post to work for the state attorney general. I'm not sure why Earl resigned. He was a good and effective senator. But once his resignation became public, Governor Ray called for a special election to fill the vacant seat and set the election date for November 6th of the same year.

Soon after, I began to think about running for office. It had been a dream of mine since the eighth grade to have a career in politics. It was just a question of finding the right opportunity. It was fortuitous that this opportunity came along when it did. I knew that being in the minority in a purple state would be an uphill battle, but I was determined to fight to realize this dream of mine.

The candidate to fill this position had to be chosen by the precinct committee representatives of District 31. I do not recall if there was a favorite of the party leaders, but it definitely wasn't me. I was black in a district that was made up of no more than twelve percent blacks. Like everyone else, I had to lobby and campaign to the precinct committee people to choose me. So, I campaigned and met with each person on the committee to convince them to support me in the race.

I was an unabashed liberal and figured that would work in my favor, as Earl Willits had also been a liberal. During the selection process, I remember we had one final debate in one of the district union halls. All of the prospective candidates gave speeches. There were around five of us. And we all spoke to the key issues of the day. My speech was pretty good. I told the delegates to the convention that, if chosen, I would focus on aid to the poor, the elderly, unemployment, and social disruption. I looked out into the audience and smiled after delivering my speech. My mother, who was living with Leala and me at the time, was there, and I noticed she was beaming alongside Leala. I was proud of me, too, as I had overcome a lot of hurdles to get to this moment in my life. I was pretty nervous about the committee's vote, but in the end, they chose me.

After being selected by the individuals on the precinct committee, the committee filed the necessary paperwork for me to represent the Democratic Party in the special election. It was finally starting to sink it. I, Thomas Mann, Jr., a black man from a family of sharecroppers in Haywood County Tennessee, had actually obtained the Democratic nomination to be a senator for the state of Iowa. I shook my head as I reflected upon my winning the nomination on the ballot to represent my party in the special election. I was one step closer to realizing another one of my life's dreams.

Campaigning

Before throwing my hat in the ring, I discussed my intention to run for public office with Leala. I let her know that I was told that I could not take a leave of absence from the ICRC to campaign, which meant I would need to resign if I wanted to run in the special election. After consulting with my wife, I stepped down as executive director of the ICRC at the age of twenty-nine and announced my intention to seek the nomination of the Democratic Party to fill the vacant state senate seat left by Earl Willits.

We knew there was no guarantee of winning and that I could be without income for a while after the election until I found a new position. Ever supportive, Leala encouraged me to run because she knew this was my life's ambition. I told Leala that, in my heart, I knew I wanted to change things. I had personal skin in the game. Having grown up in a system of sharecropping that was an institutional way of undermining the labor of people of color and preventing them from climbing the socioeconomic ladder and effectively keeping them enslaved. I lived in a time period where we were on the edge of dismantling Jim Crow, a legal and social system of menacing minorities and denying them justice. It was the beginning of a movement, and I wanted to work to contribute to the cause of racial justice. Leala said that she understood. "Tom, I know you feel deeply about this. This may be difficult, but I'll support you in it. I'll always support you." And the decision was made.

While it was exciting to be beginning a new chapter in our lives, I also knew we had our work cut out for us. But I was determined to hold on throughout the campaign and to give it my all.

My next step was to get a good team in place. Earl Willits graciously agreed to chair my campaign. His wife Martha, a precinct committee person, volunteered to serve on my campaign committee. I then hired Norma Matthews to manage my campaign. Nolden Gentry, an African American member of the Des Moines School Board, and Jerry Crawford, a prominent Des Moines attorney, were on the campaign finance committee. And my wife Leala served as campaign treasurer and all-around cheerleader.

Campaigning was hard and demanding work. I would rise every morning and have breakfast. Around 9:00 a.m., I would go to the basement and start making calls. My first call would be to Norma Matthews, my campaign manager, to discuss our plans for the day. The fact that I paid Norma for her work did not go over well with all the Democrats in Polk County. After the campaign, the Democratic Party went so far as to refuse to reimburse my campaign debt. Polk County Democrats were of the opinion that they did volunteer work and that Norma shouldn't have been paid.

Regardless of what Polk County thought about how I ran my campaign, Norma was a good manager, and I felt she deserved to be paid for all of the hard work she was doing. She was very organized and worked hard to monitor our strategy to ensure that we met our goals each day. Part of our strategy included meet and greets with constituents, known as "campaign coffees." These coffees were held during the day, and Norma handled all of the scheduling. Whenever I had these, I would plan my day around them so I could meet with my prospective constituents and learn what was most important to them.

After my morning call with Norma, I would get into a 1965 Cadillac DeVille, put campaign signs in the trunk, and ride the senate district searching for a place to put them. While I was out, I would check the signs that we'd already installed for vandalism or destruction and replace any that needed to be swapped out.

Some of the signs we used were made of plastic, which were sturdier than the ones we had made from paper stock. Most of our signs were approximately one foot by two feet. We also had some larger yard signs made of wood of varying sizes. I specifically checked these for vandalism. On occasion, they would have black paint splattered on them and need to be replaced. Black paint on my signs was a frequent occurrence. Other candidates had signs defaced, but I have no recollection of other candidates having black paint thrown on their signs.

When swapping out the signs, I would occasionally meet with voters who came out to ask about the signs and the special election, and we would talk about the campaign. It was important to me that I represented my voters, and I was interested in hearing from them, even when I was doing something as menial as installing yard signs.

After checking the signs, I would go home and retreat to the basement and handwrite thank-you notes to all the contributors to my campaign. This was the principal way my campaign was funded. It was also another means of making contacts with voters. I would give these postcards to Leala so she could mail them for me. I also spent this time reading and responding to any mail related to the campaign.

Around 3:00 or 4:00 p.m., I would go canvassing in the district. This was about the time that people would start getting home from work. I would go door to door until about 7:30 or 8:00 p.m. This was how I met most voters in the district. Sometimes, my brother Kenneth and my cousins Robert and Jesse would go with me.

When I finished canvassing for the evening, I would go home and have dinner with Leala and rest for a bit. Around 8:30 or 9:00, I went up to Mercy Hospital to see my brother Keith, who had been injured in a car accident. His neck was broken, and he was paralyzed from the chest down. I would exercise Keith's legs until about 10:00 p.m. and then head home. Visiting Keith added a little pressure to my campaign, but I was not going to abandon my brother in this time of need. He looked forward to the nightly visits. His legs were paralyzed, and I would exercise them while visiting. He and I were both thrilled on the night when he finally felt something and was able to wiggle his toes after about three months.

Once home, I would check in with Leala to see if there was any news on the campaign and then go to the basement for another couple of hours and do paperwork, retiring sometime between midnight and 1:00 a.m. And then the next day I would get up and start all over again.

As treasurer, Leala received and checked the mail for any campaign contributions. She recorded these contributions and created the official campaign finance reports, showing the contributors and their respective amounts. There were very few computers in 1979, so she did all of these entries by hand. It was tedious work, but she was happy to do it. Leala also attended coffees and meetings on behalf of the campaign, made phone calls, and accepted yard sign locations. There were no cell phones in 1979, so this was all done from our home campaign headquarters.

Gary Baugher

The Republicans selected Gary Baugher, a Republican who self-identified as more of a Libertarian, to run against me in the special election. My district had produced the last two girls' high school basketball champions. Baugher sought to make six-player girls' basketball versus five-player girls' basketball an issue. I had criticized the six-player girls' high school basketball as discriminatory, since colleges played five-player basketball, which placed these players at a disadvantage when applying for college scholarships. Initially, I did not think my position would be an issue. However, our senate district was deep in basketball country, and I quickly learned that it was something many constituents were passionate about. Two state championships had recently been won by high school girls living in the district, which included the rural areas of Saylorville and Ankeny. In spite of Baugher's focus on girls' basketball and my unfavorable position, I continued to focus on employment and economic-related issues, which I felt were more pressing. District 31 was composed of principally Democratic voters, and I was hoping this would work in my favor.

Gary was a cordial candidate. He and I got along well throughout the campaign. We just disagreed on the critical issues of unemployment and abortion, as well as his stance on girls' basketball. It was a fair campaign as far as I could tell. He did raise my position on six-player basketball during our debates, but that wasn't surprising as part of District 31 and Baugher's home was in Ankeny, which had a really good girls' basketball team.

We had at least two debates: One was in Ankeny and the other was in Des Moines. The unemployment rate was high in the fall of 1979, and Roe v. Wade was still a controversial ruling, having been decided just six years prior. So, unemployment and abortion rights were both hot issues during our debates. I was for abortion and decreasing the unemployment rate; whereas, Baugher was pro-life and felt there should be less government intervention when it came to employment and other issues.

I also campaigned for public education. Determination and perseverance got me off the farm back when I was a teenager, but it was public education that opened the door for me. It was something I was very passionate about, as I wanted others to be afforded the same opportunities that I was. The poor and disadvantaged, especially blacks and other minorities, need a good education if they want to be able to advance financially and socially. Without an education, it is difficult to care for yourself and your family and to buy life's essentials, such as clothing, food, shelter, and reliable transportation to get to and from work. I believed in public education and argued for it. Baugher also supported education, but the teacher's union ended up supporting me in the election because my talking points were stronger, as I had lived it and was proof of what a good education could do.

November 6th, 1979

After three straight months of campaigning, election day had finally arrived. I remember feeling proud as I cast my vote on November 6th, 1979. Leala and I went together to vote at 9:00 a.m. in our precinct. After we cast our ballots, we drove to the other precincts to check on the activity to get a sense for what was happening. I was a bundle of nerves as we all gathered in my basement and waited for the returns that evening. Like any race, it felt like a nail-biter. And since this was my very first campaign, I was especially nervous. It was comforting to have my wife and family and members of my campaign all there with me.

Unfortunately, after all the votes had been counted, Baugher had garnered 3,261 votes, or sixty-three percent of the vote, to my 1,916 votes. When the race had been called, I phoned my opponent to concede the election and to congratulate him on his win. My friends, family, and campaign team were all supportive and encouraged me to stick with it. They reminded me that I had a good platform and that with more time to prepare and campaign and to win over more of the constituents, we would have a better shot.

I nodded and thanked everyone for their kind words as I reflected on the campaign. I had campaigned throughout the district, going door-to-door. That's probably what beat me more than anything else. I was black, and Baugher was white. I could see no other significant factor. As I was campaigning and spoke with the constituents in my district, there was a part of me that wondered if I was going to lose the race because of this, but I held on, determined to stick it out. Earl Willits later told me, "There wasn't a dime's worth of difference in my position on the issues" from his (in a liberal district that he won repeatedly), which only confirmed my suspicions.

After the election, I learned that Donald Rowan, a lobbyist for the Iowa Federation of Labor, said that a black man could not win an election in Iowa. I liked and respected Mr. Rowan, but I have to admit that I was disappointed when I heard that he was closing the door on blacks seeking public office in Iowa. I would likely have run again, regardless, but I was not going to have prominent democrats like Rowan citing me as the basis for denying blacks the opportunity to seek office in perpetuity.

In one sense, he can be credited for underscoring my desire to run again. I was not going to be held out as the reason that no black person could seek office in Iowa ever again. Just like the incident with my elementary school classmate, I wasn't going to let go. I was going to run again and do everything I could to win.

Chapter 6

New Beginnings

After climbing a great hill, one only finds that there are many more hills to climb.

— *Nelson Mandela*

Social Scars

It was a hard blow not winning the Iowa State Senate race in the special election back in November of 1979. We had all worked hard, and I did my best to represent my district. Unfortunately, it was not enough to convince the voters, and I lost my first state senate race to Republican opponent Gary Baugher. Because I was not allowed to stay on as director of the ICRC while campaigning, I had been out of work since October of 1979. After the election, I sat at home feeling lost, wondering what my next move would be.

While I conceded the loss, looking back it's understandable that I would second-guess myself and my abilities as I went over the events leading up to the election. I was taught to feel inferior by the circumstances that my family and I lived in when we were growing up. As kids, we were raised to despise being black and to be deferential to whites. It was just the way things were, and we didn't question it. As a result, there was this great loss of cultural pride and dignity that affected all of us, like a virus.

Many mixed-race blacks passed for whites and were afforded certain privileges, such as eating where they wanted to eat in public places, sleeping in decent hotels, not being derided or called the N-word, having the right to vote, and just generally being treated like a first-class citizen instead of a second-class one.

While I knew the difference between being black and passing for white, I never personally knew anyone who actually passed for white. I remember as kids, we would play and taunt each other with the following ditty: "If you're white, you're alright. If you're black, get back. If you're brown, stick around." At the time, we didn't realize that we were being taught to feel inferior and that our ditties were reinforcing this. We were asleep to this societal programming. Nevertheless, it was happening to each of us. Daily.

We were being indoctrinated into a place of insecurity and self-loathing by a sometimes silent and pernicious enemy that often included ourselves. We insulted each other by chiding our friends for having nappy hair and calling each other racial slurs and singing the ditty about skin color and societal privilege. I can see now that we helped to perpetuate these stereotypes. However, we did not create them. We simply parroted what we heard and learned from others. Unfortunately, the insecurities and self-doubts from our childhood often left deep and permanent scars.

But scars can also serve a purpose. They can paralyze or harm you and others if you remain unaware of them, or they can serve as a catalyst to fight back if you awaken to their perils. Fortunately, one day my eyes began to open. By the time I was in middle school, I began to understand that something was deeply wrong with the way we treated each other and the way others treated us, and I wanted to do something about it. I wanted to make things right for myself and other minorities.

So, I started reading the papers. And to get the word out, I also sold a small newspaper known as *Grit*. I sold this paper door-to-door and had to walk miles to do so. I also watched the news on TV and had conversations about what was going on in our community. I spent time discussing the social issues of the day with family members—especially my aunts Annette, Arnette, and Suzette—while picking cotton and reflecting on the impact these issues were having on our lives. I also had discussions with my friend Larry Grimes and with Earnest Ellison, a classmate in my West High School class who had the second highest grades.

After taking some time to process the news and the discussions I was having with others, I concluded that all of the significant decision makers in my community were lawyers. It was then that I decided that I wanted to be a civil rights attorney so I could fight against the social injustices of my day and help other minorities have a fair shake in life. I also had enough self-awareness to know that if I was going to succeed, I would have to work harder than my lighter-skinned counterparts to prove myself worthy of the challenge.

Tom Miller

The year before the special election, Tom Miller, a democrat, ran for Iowa's attorney general and won. After losing my first senate race, I sat out for a couple of months. During this period, Leala and I discussed our options. More specifically, my options. Leala had worked as a Hearing Officer at the Iowa Department of Job Service from 1977 to 1978 and was currently working as a Supervising Attorney at the Polk County Legal Aid Society. So, we had income coming in, and it wasn't all bleak.

While I was disappointed about losing the election, after sitting around and discussing my options with Leala, we decided I should try working for the state government again. We considered the possibility of opening up a private law practice where we and other attorneys could work, but it takes a while to build up a practice, and we knew it would be best to have some additional income coming in now, especially with plans to start a family soon. While we were both licensed attorneys, neither Leala nor I were primarily motivated by money. But I was motivated by my desire for service, and I knew that I could be of best service working for the state.

So, in January of 1980, I approached Tom Miller about returning to the state attorney general's office for work. I did not know Tom Miller that well, but I knew Earl Willits who had chaired my campaign. Since Earl was now working as an assistant attorney general, I reached out to him. I do not think there was an actual vacancy; however, based on Willits' recommendation, Attorney General Miller made room for me. After my interview, I was hired back as an assistant attorney general and provided legal and trial counsel for the state mental health agencies and the Department of Corrections. While representing the Department of Social Services in prison-related civil rights litigation, I wrote informal AG opinions. Informal AG opinions are informal opinions on legal matters issued by Assistant Attorney Generals. Formal opinions are usually issued under the signature of the Attorney General and represent official policy of the state.

The Second Time Around

Working for Miller was more business-like than my experience working for Richard Turner, the previous attorney general. The atmosphere in Miller's office was more formal and less jocular. With the Criminal Appeals crowd, there was a good deal of joking around and camaraderie. I did what I considered to be good work for Criminal Appeals back when I worked for Turner, but I also participated in the mirth-making with my colleagues.

While we were cordial in the Social Services Division under Miller, we were also very focused on doing the work.

During my first tour at the attorney general's office in the mid-seventies, I worked challenging cases in Criminal Appeals, although not initially. Back then, I was afforded a certain amount of time to ramp up and get acquainted with all the different types of cases, and they started me off with easier cases so I could get the hang of things. In Social Services, however, it was more of an "all-hands-on-deck" atmosphere. Despite the fact that there was less camaraderie than my early days in Turner's office, I was back in my element and thriving.

All in all, it was good to be back and working for the state. Some of my early cases required me to represent mental health institutions. Under Miller, I tried several cases in federal court involving mental health issues. To do this, I had to interpret the mental health statutes, including many issues of first impression. I remember working on an important case for the Department of Corrections, Watson v. Ray, with another Assistant Attorney General, Bruce McDonald. This case challenged the constitutionality of the conditions of Iowa's prisons. The Watson case lasted for over a month and had numerous witnesses. Bruce and I shared the duties in that case, with Bruce taking the lead.

I also litigated numerous cases involving the prison conditions against inmates. These cases challenged such areas as inmate disciplinary actions, the quality of the food and lack of sanitary conditions in state prisons, and the offering of healthcare for inmates. And I handled cases involving the medical care for patients inside mental health institutions, including the quality of patient care, medical coverage, discharge protocols, and the length of voluntary commitment.

When working for Attorney General Miller, my supervisor was John Black. John assigned me to work for the state prisons and mental health institutions, but he did not typically assign me specific cases to work on. The exception was Watson v. Ray. John had asked me to assist Bruce since it was a large, high-profile case. Generally, however, the workload came about when institutions were sued, or questions arose that required my help. Then any new cases specific to my area were directed to me by the administrative staff.

There was a good group of assistant attorneys general in Miller's office at the time. We were dedicated and up for any challenge that came our way. Stephen Robinson was an experienced attorney who managed a full caseload while availing himself to others, whenever his expertise was needed. Jonathan Golden and Candy Morgan also had pretty full plates and impressive track records to match, as did Craig Brenneise, Layne Lindebak, Brent Hege, and Patricia Hulting. Mostly, I worked independently in Social Services. While I maintained contact with my former colleagues in Criminal Appeals, including Robbins, Dryer, and McGrane, Leala's contact with the Criminal Appeals crew was limited after she left in 1977 as she had lost touch with them after she went to work for the Iowa Department of Job Service.

Thunder Child

Soon after starting my new job with the state, our first daughter Nari was born. Leala and I had been wanting to start a family since we had married in 1976, but we decided to wait a few years so we could get settled into our new jobs. After the special election, we decided the time was right, and in early 1980, we were excited to learn that we were expecting and let our family and friends know about this exciting news.

The best that I can recall, Leala had an uneventful pregnancy. In fact, during her third trimester, we took a weeklong trip to San Juan, Puerto Rico. Leala and I rented a car and drove about the island to take in the sights, including the fort at Old San Juan. Driving around the countryside, we marveled at how small things seemed when compared to what we were familiar with back home in Des Moines and were surprised when we stumbled upon a McDonald's. During our trip, it was pretty warm and humid, a welcome change from the cold back home. Perhaps this trip to San Juan sparked Nari's interest in world travel. She is a big travel buff, having visited England, Romania, Portugal, Jamaica, Costa Rica, and Cancun, as well as over twenty U.S. states since her first trip in utero.

While Leala's pregnancy was uneventful, the delivery was another story altogether. When Leala started going into labor, I drove her to Des Moines General Hospital, which was about twenty minutes from our home. Leala was in labor for forty-two consecutive hours. It was a difficult birth for Leala. We like to say that is because Nari is stubborn, and she was born when she was good and ready. Fortunately, I pressed the doctors, and they gave Leala an epidural of Demerol after thirty-eight hours for the pain. I remember Leala had the shakes for an hour after delivery, and she was in the hospital for four days to recover from the event. I stayed by Leala's side during the entire labor and made sure she was comfortable during her stay.

We were blessed to have Nari arrive in November of 1980. She came into this world weighing six pounds, twelve and a half ounces and was born two weeks early. Leala and I sometimes joke that Nari came early because she didn't want to miss out on anything. To this day, Nari is eager to be involved in family events and has a strong spirit, living up to her namesake, which means "thunder child" in Japanese.

Once Nari was born, Leala received congratulatory calls from her sister, Joyce Earvin, and our friends Jim Robbins, David Dryer, and Carol and Robert Oberbillig. We also received a generous outpouring of baby gifts from friends, neighbors, family, and coworkers when we brought Nari home. After four days in the hospital, Leala and Nari were allowed to come home. Nari slept quietly in her bassinet for the first month. By the time she was eight months old, she was sleeping through the night, which we both appreciated. Leala and I shared diaper duty and taking care of Nari. I got the hang of it pretty quickly. We took turns changing Nari late at night, and I got pretty good at changing diapers while half-asleep.

I took a few weeks off from work to be with Leala, and Leala took a few months off before she returned to work. Once we were both at work, my mother helped take care of Nari. I remember being pretty tired when I did return to work. I wasn't a big coffee drinker, but I tried to stomach it back then. Nevertheless, I still had difficulty keeping my eyes open at work during those first eight months or so after Nari's birth.

Overall, Nari was a contented baby and easily satisfied. I remember her favorite things at that age were sucking her thumb and grabbing Leala's hair. Her first word was "baby" at ten months. She was a bright baby, and as she grew older, we nicknamed her "bad baby" because she got into quite a bit of mischief and because she balked at toilet training and mimicked whatever we said, which was cute, but sometimes wearing.

While she was moody at two years old, Nari grew into a studious kid. Leala and I both were thrilled at how well she had taken to her studies, as we had worked hard to instill the importance and value of a good education for both of our daughters. Nari finished high school at the Texas Academy of Math and Science and graduated from Stanford University with a degree in Computer Science, which she used in her position at Hewlett Packard where she worked as a computer engineer.

Moving On

While I enjoyed the work I was doing for the state attorney general, after working as an assistant attorney general for just over two and a half years and settling into my new parenting role, the call to serve in public office beckoned, once again. After talking things over with Leala, I decided I would try another run for state senate in August of 1982. We both felt I was ready and that I would have a better shot the second time around. I shared my decision to run for office with my colleague John Black and my boss Attorney General Miller, who were both supportive of my decision. Because of the uproar over my hiring Norma Matthews during the first campaign, I decided against hiring a campaign manager for my second run for office. I did, however, feel it was important to have someone I could trust to chair my campaign. Someone who would be just as dedicated as I was. Someone who would help me run a fair and effective campaign. Every time I sat down to think it over, I kept thinking of the man Norma suggested, Tom Parkins. While I didn't know him that well, Norma said he would give everything he had to the campaign. I had a good feeling about things as I picked up the phone to give him a call. Now that I had some more experience under my belt, it seemed like we might actually have a shot at winning a state seat and make history in the process.

Chapter 7

The Call to Serve

Our greatest weakness lies in giving up. The most certain way to succeed is always to try just one more time.
— Thomas Edison

Find a Campaign Chair

As I picked up the phone to dial my prospective campaign chair, I looked at the clock on the kitchen wall. It was almost noon on a Saturday. I'd waited a few hours to make the call in case Tom Parkins was one of those who slept in on weekends. But by now I figured he'd be up. I glanced down at my notes on the kitchen table. I was ready. Norma was an excellent judge of character. She wouldn't steer me wrong. I took a deep breath and gathered my courage. You got this, I told myself, as I began to dial.

As I waited for someone to answer, I studied my notes. I had all the stats ready to share with Tom. It almost felt like I was preparing for a case. I'd spent time researching the important issues and was prepared to share facts with Tom about my district as well as any precedents from previous elections.

On the third ring, I heard a gentleman answer.

"Hello."

"Hello, Mr. Parkins?"

"Yes."

"This is Tom Mann, assistant attorney general for the state of Iowa."

"Oh, hello. How are you?"

"I'm fine, thank you. How are you?"

"I'm good, thanks."

I nodded, relieved. He seemed very personable on the phone.

"Glad to hear it. Listen, Norma Matthews suggested I give you a call. I don't know if you remember, but she ran my campaign during the special election back in '79."

"Oh, yes. The Willits seat, right?"

Norma was right. Parkins was sharp as a tack. I shuffled the papers on the kitchen table and leaned in closer to the receiver.

"Yes. I've given it some thought, and I've decided to run for state senate again this year and was wondering if you had a few minutes to chat with me about my campaign…"

I could feel my body relax into the chair a little as we exchanged pleasantries. We had a good chat, and he said he was interested in helping me out. He said he would need to talk things over with his wife first and get back to me, but it all sounded very positive. I made a mental note to call Norma later to thank her for the referral.

Looking back on that phone call I made in January of 1982, I remember being pretty nervous. I didn't really know Tom that well, and I was asking a pretty big favor. He was the former Chair of the Polk County Democratic Party. Having lost a previous senate race, I needed to persuade him that my running was not a lost cause. I decided I would bring up the low voter turnout in the 1979 special election and share what I felt would help to boost turnout this time. I also wanted to address the fact of my ethnicity over the phone without insulting Tom, who was a white man and might not fully understand what it was like to be discriminated against based on the color of your skin. In essence, I wanted him to know what he was getting into, in case the opposition defaced our signs like they did last time or pulled other tactics. I also felt it was fair that he knew that race could play a role in the campaign and that blacks were a minority in this district. He also might have some suggestions on how we could target minority voters in this election, so I wanted to put everything on the table for him.

During the call I also gave him some statistical data from the district. I wanted to assuage any concerns he might have had, so I mentioned that in previous elections, Democratic candidates in our district fared very well. For example, over sixty percent of the votes went to Democratic candidates in recent elections, granting the wins to Attorney General Tom Miller and to U.S. Senators John Culver and Dick Clark. So, I felt it was important to focus our efforts on the Democratic base so we could improve voter turnout in this next election.

Our district, 43, had been reapportioned and revised. It was composed of the Saylor precincts and some other precincts from the former District 31. This new district was still leaning Democratic, and I mentioned that it was the fourth largest Democratic district in the state so that Tom would know we would have a strong, built-in demographic. The latest polls had 52.2% of the constituents as registered Democrats and nineteen percent as Independents, which could work in our favor.

Overall, the district was composed of 12.7% blacks and 83.9% whites. Other minorities made up the remaining 3.4%. I shared that our target demographic was anyone between eighteen and sixty-four years of age and that these voters were homeowners, making just over 10K per year. Tom listened attentively and asked poignant questions. As I mentioned the obstacles that we encountered during the last campaign, I simultaneously strove to convince him that no one would work harder than I would during this campaign, and that my platform would appeal to the majority of the district.

Building the Rest of Our Team

Because of the uproar over my hiring Norma Matthews during the first campaign, I did not hire a campaign manager for the second campaign. Fortunately, I was able to persuade Tom to chair my campaign, and we got to work soon after. My good friend and coworker Brent Hege also agreed to work with me. While he didn't want a title, Brent was effectively working as my campaign coordinator, and the three of us essentially ran the campaign.

I'd worked with Brent at the attorney general's office, and it was nice having him on my team when I ran for state senate again. In the months ahead, he'd end up spending nearly as much time as I had in my basement working on the campaign. He was invaluable to me as a strategist and as a friend. This was his first campaign, but he was a fast learner, and he believed in my vision. He would come to my place after work and spend time with me responding to any issues that had arisen. He also supervised the phone banks and helped create the questionnaire that we used for it. It was good to run ideas by him, and he was a true asset when it came to dealing with any unforeseen issues.

Once I had Tom and Brent on board, the three of us started looking over the demographics of our district and began to form a campaign strategy. During our planning sessions, we considered every angle and possibility. Like the prior campaign, we decided we would focus on our base of Democratic voters. To increase voter turnout, Tom also wanted us to make at least six different contacts with our voters. To bring this about, we would go door-to-door, hold coffees, fundraise, hold phone banks (at both the beginning and the end of the campaign), and put up and maintain yard

74

signs. Tom's theory was that a voter could be persuaded with just six contacts, so we worked diligently to ensure that we reached that magic number during the campaign.

Leala served as treasurer and collected the mail like she did last time. She also created all of the campaign finance reports. She worked her regular job during the day. And in the evenings, she sat in with Brent and I at home to help out with campaign strategy. She also kept me in check as a father and made sure I carved out time each evening at 8:00 to spend with Nari, which entailed reading to her and helping her get ready for bed, something that I enjoyed doing and was grateful to Leala for making sure I kept both feet on the ground as a candidate, spouse, and father.

As with most candidates, I did most of the heavy lifting on the fundraising. I mailed fundraising letters and postcards to my constituents. The letter I wrote was typewritten and showcased my qualifications for the position as well as the issues I would take a stand on for my constituents. We made thousands of copies of this letter so we could send out a mass mailing to our constituents early in the campaign. I also handwrote twenty-five to thirty postcards every night after Brent and I had discussed the days' events and mapped out what we would do the following day. I did this for three consecutive months while working full-time at the attorney general's office. It wore me out, and some days it was hard to stay awake at work, but somehow I pulled through. Looking back, I probably mailed close to 2,000 postcards during that time. While we did not actively seek money from political action committees (PACs), we certainly accepted all donations. We raised approximately $11,000 that year, which was sufficient for a state senate election back then.

My family members were all supportive and eager to help. They volunteered whenever they had time. My brother Kenneth Maclin and my cousins Robert Maclin and Jesse

Currie would sometimes canvass with me. My mom's apartment was about three to four blocks from our home, so it was convenient to have her so close by. She would babysit Nari whenever she could, but most of the time we placed Nari in daycare with a neighbor, Linda Cummings. And later on, we ended up placing her in La Petite Academy, both of which were on Lower Beaver Road.

Nari has always been a helper. When we were making signs for the '82 campaign, she liked to hang out in the garage with us. She was mostly in the way, but I loved it. It was a true delight having her around, wanting to help in any way that she could. She would often watch as we stapled the signs to the stake and would try to talk to us while we were working. We used commercially made yard signs and paid a printer to paint most of our signs, which we stapled to a stake with a heavy-duty stapler. Nari couldn't handle the stapler, but she could hand me a sign or a stake and would often squeal with delight whenever she had a job that she could do.

We also had some larger wooden signs, but they were hand-painted by volunteers with steadier eyes and hands than mine. In addition to getting help with signage, we had some canvassers and volunteers that we recruited to participate in our phone banks. In total, we had about forty people working on the campaign. Brent and I worked almost daily in my basement, while the other volunteers worked whenever they could contribute their time.

Primary Season

I qualified for the primary election by filling out the paperwork and obtaining the requisite signatures on my candidacy papers from my constituents. The state primary began in March of 1982 and ended in June of that same year. Brent and I coordinated campaigns with two of the other representative candidates in the district, Florence Buhr and Gary Sherzan. I carried yard signs for my campaign and for Florence's campaign in the trunk of my car and carried a heavy-duty stapler and repaired yard signs for their campaigns, as well as mine, when we were out canvassing.

Aside from helping the other candidates with their signs, we ran the campaign pretty much as if I was the only candidate. We did the usual door-to-door campaigning and targeted the precincts with a heavy percentage of black voters to increase voter turnout. We decided to canvass in the neighborhoods where I thought that I would be accepted. I fervently believed that I was the best qualified candidate when it came down to education and experience. It could have all been ego, but I was ready to win.

This was a different strategy from my first campaign. While I had campaigned in some of the predominantly black precincts during the first campaign, I made them a target during the second campaign. The theory was that every vote from those precincts was going to be a vote for me. So, I worked to turn out every voter in those key areas. Our efforts paid off because on June 8th, 1982, I won forty-three percent of the vote in the four-way Democratic primary, which gave me a win of seventeen points over my closest opponent. We were heartened by this victory and used this to fuel our efforts for the upcoming election in November.

Bobby Baker was the supported union candidate during the 1982 primary campaign. AFL-CIO, the labor union in the district, was strong and favored Bobby over the other candidates. While the union supported Baker during the primary, I was a strong union advocate as well and was able to garner their support after winning the primary.

Campaign Strategies

After winning the primary, I thought I had a really good shot at the senate seat. The district was over fifty percent Democratic, and we had a sound strategy and the volunteers to execute it.

Additionally, my positions on the issues were good for the district. Unemployment was high at around twelve percent, and it was double that for the black population.

Canvassing played a big role in our campaign. This was something that all of us were involved in. Early on, I reached out to one of my fraternity brother from the University of Iowa, Jim McCown, to see if he would like to be involved. He was a close friend and happily volunteered. Soon after Jim joined our team, he and I went door-to-door to meet with our constituents. I think our constituents enjoyed meeting directly with us and having a chance to voice their concerns as well as their support.

We received additional help from the Iowa State Democratic Party. They assigned a state party staffer, Kevin Bolden, to work with my campaign right after I won the primary. Kevin was also a fraternity brother, so he fit right in. Both Kevin and Jim lived in the district. As did Sam Wilson, another campaign volunteer and fraternity brother.

Jim also helped out with the phone banks and made calls. The phone banks helped get my message out and also solicited enthusiastic supporters for small contributions. Iowa Realty was a well-known supporter to Democratic campaigns back then. Because of this, Tom and Brent approached them about our campaign to see if we could use some of their offices to run our phone banks. Iowa Realty had several locations in Des Moines and graciously offered up three or four of their offices for our volunteers to use to call our constituents.

We'd make phone calls after work, typically from 4:00 p.m. to 8:00 p.m. We started with a small crew of about ten people and began calling voters in the district, which consisted of 31,198 voters. We called all voters, Democrats, Republicans, and Independents. We called them at least twice during the campaign season, making just over 31,000 calls during the first round, and another 31,000 or so during the second round, for a total of over 62,000 calls. Something we could not have done without the assistance from Iowa Realty or the volunteers who generously gave of their time at the phone banks.

Signage was also important in maintaining a strong presence in our district. To cut down on maintenance, we used plastic yard signs as opposed to the paper or cardboard yard signs that we used in the last campaign. While we called all of the voters, we did not canvass as hard in Saylor or other parts of the district that were unfavorable to me. Instead, we decided to target our canvassing to Democratic precincts that we suspected would support me. And we followed the same strategy with our signs, taking care to place them in prime areas throughout the district.

Like the last campaign, our basement was campaign headquarters. The phone banks were paying off, as we were able to support and obtain donations this way. I also wrote articles for the local newspaper and sent thank you notes for every contribution we received, regardless of the amount. Brent would phone the lead volunteers of the phone bank at the end of the day to go over how things went. At night, Brent and I would discuss the results of the day's phone banking efforts and make adjustments to our questionnaire as needed.

We generally asked voters if they had voted in the district previously and if they had chosen a candidate and who that candidate was. We also asked them what issues were most important to them. Other questions included whether or not they had heard of my campaign and if they had a favorable impression or unfavorable impression of my campaign. If it was favorable, we asked if they were planning to vote for me and if they would like to make a donation to the campaign at this time.

We also held coffees at the homes of our constituents. We found them through the phone banks, and if they were supportive of the campaign, we asked if they would be willing to host a coffee. The coffees were generally held during the day, so primarily homemakers and neighbors would attend. Typically, there would be around eight to ten people at these events where we served coffee and cookies. If I could not make a coffee, Leala would go as a surrogate. The attendees at the coffees were very attentive. They would listen to a presentation about the issues of the day, such as the high unemployment and inflation rates, and then ask questions. Like most Iowans, they were apprised of the issues and raised intelligent questions.

We all worked hard during the campaign. I campaigned every day, including Saturday and Sunday. I canvassed after work from 5:00 p.m. to 8:00 p.m. I would sleep in on the weekends and then get started around 10:00 a.m. and work on the campaign until about 10:00 or so in the evenings. While tired from working two jobs, I never missed a hearing, but I did put my head down on my desk at work sometimes. Whenever I was tired and appeared to be falling asleep, the secretary would bring me some additional work, which helped me stay awake.

A Dirty Campaign

During the special election to fill Earl Willits' seat in 1979, both sides ran a fair campaign. While we didn't always see eye to eye on every issue, the Republican candidate Gary Baugher and I had a cordial relationship during and after the campaign. On occasion, I would visit the state capitol and see him when he was serving. I wanted to maintain good relations with him in the event that I joined him in the senate after the next election. Unfortunately, he lost his run for re-election to William Palmer of Ankeny, so we didn't have the opportunity to work together, but I enjoyed our meetings and the opportunity to learn the ropes during the campaign I ran against him.

The general election of 1982 was an entirely different matter. Jo Ann Trucano was the Republican candidate. Unfortunately, Trucano and her team ran a dirty campaign. While there was no bad press, the opposition threw black paint on my yard signs and distributed pictures of me that were distorted to make me look like a convict. These pictures were posted on fliers all over the district.

While I did not see Trucano with any black paint, I did see the distorted, convict-looking pictures of me that her campaign distributed throughout the district whenever I was out. During our daily runs to check on our yard signs or when we were canvassing, I found the offensive pictures sticking out of constituent mailboxes or displayed on their lawns and took them down.

I did call the *Des Moines Register* when paint was thrown on my signs, but the *Register* was of the opinion that it was just general dirty campaign tricks. So, I stopped calling and just worked hard and focused on my campaign. I knew the district, and I knew the issues. In addition to leaning Democratic, it was a union district. Running on the High Fives of high inflation, high interest rates, high unemployment, high taxes, and the high cost of living, I knew I was a strong candidate, so I was not going to allow the opposition to intimidate me.

Whenever we saw the damage, we would pick up the fliers and repair our signs. At times it felt like we couldn't keep up, but we did our best to clean up after them. While I could not prove it was Trucano doing this since I never saw her throw paint or distribute the fliers, I knew that I and members of my campaign were not distributing these fliers or defacing my signs. Along with gerrymandering and voter suppression, defacing candidate signs and distributing offensive campaign literature about the opposing party is a regular Republican tactic, even today.

In spite of the smear campaign, I persevered and stayed focused on my platform. In addition to the High Fives, I supported Roe v. Wade, which appealed to the Democratic base. Whereas, Trucano was running a textbook Republican campaign and was against a women's right to choose and was more focused on lowering taxes and reducing the government's reach, which translated into less state assistance for constituents. Unemployment and public education were big issues during my campaign. When we approached the teacher's union and shared our views on public education, they gladly supported my campaign. It felt good to have them in our court, along with the support of the labor union, with all the attempts by the opposition to discredit our campaign.

Leaving the Farm Behind

It was always my ambition to be a public servant. By the time I was in the eighth grade, I had determined that farm work was not for me. Picking cotton was back-breaking work. A cotton sack was anywhere from six to nine feet long. You had to hang it across your shoulders and stoop over, pulling the cotton from the bolls. If the weight of the cotton didn't break your back, the matured bolls would cut and rip your fingers. Picking okra was even worse. You could stand up straight when you picked okra, but the okra would cut right through your fingers if you weren't wearing gloves. This was problematic for me because I hated the gloves. They reeked from the smell of the slimy okra. But I hated getting cut even worse, so I'd wear them begrudgingly.

Fortunately, I was able to leave the farm behind for college. And now, after spending eight years in government service, I had positioned myself to run for state office. I firmly believed that a policy maker would offer me the best chance of bettering my life and helping other people. And with my wife's support and that of the rest of my campaign team, I was going to try my best to make that happen.

I had learned from the last campaign and felt that my experience and education gave me a leg up on the other Democrats who ran against me in the primary election. Having worked as an assistant attorney general and as the director of the ICRC, I felt confident and qualified for the role of state senator. I also felt our new district would work in our favor. While District 43 did not mirror District 31, it was very similar. And even though Trucano had defeated Democrat Norman Jesse in the house race in this same district in 1980, it was a small margin of just 133 votes. The phone banking and canvassing let me harmonize my views with the constituents in my district. I took a compassionate approach to governing: I was in favor of energy assistance for the elderly, increased support for education, more community corrections programs, and improved job-training programs. Given the high inflation and unemployment rate, I also felt that the next legislative session would be dominated by the economy, so I supported tax incentives for small-business owners to encourage them to create new jobs for the community.

Taking Leave

During the primary season, I was able to work and campaign in the evenings. I also continued to write informal opinions during this time for the attorney general. After winning the primary election, however, I took a leave of absence from my position as assistant attorney general. Jonathan Golden, another assistant attorney general, represented the mental health agencies during my absence.

In August of 1982, I returned from leave to finish up my work. My final informal opinion pertained to the question of which county had to pay a mental health patient's legal settlement for inpatient care. Once I completed this work, I resigned from my position as an assistant attorney general so that I could campaign full-time for the fall election.

During the campaign, Leala and I discussed our options and decided that we would open a joint private law practice after the election, regardless of the outcome. While I enjoyed the work I did for the attorney general, I felt it was time to move on. And because the annual stipend of $20,000 for a state senator was not enough to live off of, I would need to continue to practice law to generate some additional income for me and my family.

Leala also wanted to get into private practice. While we were both dedicated to public service, we were both attorneys and looking to be free to exercise independent judgment. There is always some limitation on that when you work for someone else. For example, when working for Tom Miller, I ran up a large research bill. Electronic research had just become available through Westlaw and Lexis-Nexis. Because of the convenience and novelty of electronic research, I relied on it a little too often instead of hitting the books in the library, as was the custom. Pretty soon, I ran up a bill and was confronted on this, which made me uncomfortable. I enjoyed using the available technology and felt that we should be allowed to use it if it supported our work. In the end, we decided that working in our own shop would be better than working in someone else's, so we decided to open the law offices of Mann & Mann in December of 1982.

Soon after I left the attorney general's office, Dianne Munns was hired to represent the mental health agencies. I relinquished the Watson v. Ray case to Bruce McDonald who wrote the post-trial brief and did all of the finishing work on this case. It was then that I was able to focus the bulk of my energy on the campaign. Brent continued to work for the attorney general after the campaign, and we remained friends until I left Iowa in 1992.

Waiting Out the Returns

On November 3rd, 1982, after months of campaigning, it was time to finally cast our votes and await the returns. Leala and I went to the polls together. I felt proud casting my vote that day as I reflected on the past months we had all put into the campaign and the journey I had taken to get there. Later that evening, Leala and I went to the Hotel Kirkwood to wait out the returns. The Kirkwood is a nice hotel located in downtown Des Moines. I had butterflies in my stomach but was also excited to find out the results after so many months of hard work and planning.

At the hotel, Leala and I gathered with Tom Parkins, Brent Hege, Sam Wilson (a fraternity brother), my brother Derek Maclin, and my cousin Joey Rawls, Jr. There were lots of other people at our hotel suite as well. Some from the campaign, some from other campaigns, and some from the public. We were all on pins and needles as we watched the returns on the television in our suite. In my mind, I kept flashing back to the past election and worrying that I would lose again. Leala would squeeze my hand whenever she sensed I was growing nervous. It was a comfort to have her by my side. My mom had offered to take care of Nari that evening, so we could attend the event at the hotel.

Around 10:00 the final results were in. I held my breath as they announced that I had won the state senate seat by garnering fifty-seven percent of the votes. Everyone cheered, and we all went to the large assembly room in the hotel for my acceptance speech. There were many people there, including the media. During my speech, I thanked everyone for their hard work and dedication to the campaign and to let them all know that I was ready to step into my new role and that I would work hard to make them all proud.

Democrats did well overall that year, winning ten of thirteen seats in Polk County. I felt I was right for the district and so were the other Democrats, and the election confirmed it. This election would mean good government for the people. Not just good officials, but a chance to bring about substantial change.

Leala and I left the hotel about 11:00 that evening and returned home. I got up late the next day and received congratulatory calls. My mom stopped by with Nari later in the day to congratulate us on the win. I was grinning ear to ear, very pleased to have won. While elated, I also knew that it was going to be difficult to achieve solutions to the unemployment problems facing the district. I had promised my constituents that I would work to solve these problems, but there were thirty other senators and a Republican governor that I would have to convince. It was going to be difficult, but I was ready for the challenge.

Chapter 8

The Fight for Human Needs

Love means hating and fighting the injustices of the world. It means having a desire to see peace and equality for all people. On a limited basis, love means caring for people close to you—your spouse, family, and friends. On a much broader basis, love means caring for your fellow man.
— Thomas J. Mann, Jr.

Sworn In

After being elected to the Iowa State Senate in November of 1982, I was looking forward to learning what my committee assignments in the new senate would be. There was little paperwork to be prepared and signed beforehand, so I spent the next two months helping Leala in her law practice, something I would continue throughout my two-term tenure in the senate.

Leala had opened a law office with Linda Pettit, a coworker from Legal Aid, earlier that year. Their office was at 25th and University in the heart of Drake University in Des Moines. Leala practiced general law; whereas, Linda was a civil rights attorney. To help pass the time, I handled a few bankruptcy cases and did some general office work.

Around January 6th of the following year, the new senate session started. My house was fifteen miles or so from the capitol, and it took me about half an hour to drive and park in the lot reserved for legislators and staff, adjacent to the capitol building. On that day, I walked proudly into the state capitol and was sworn in with the other new senators. No one from my family was present. However, I was given a new bible for the swearing in. It felt tremendous. In my mind, I had made it.

After the swearing in, a woman in a neatly pressed suit approached me.

"Senator Mann?"

I smiled. It was the first time I'd been called that.

"Yes," I said as I extended my hand.

"Marie Thayer. Very pleased to meet you."

As we shook hands, Marie, then secretary of the senate, smiled and shared that she would be giving me a quick tour of the offices. I appreciated having someone to show me around on my first day and was in awe of the architecture and beauty of the capitol building. After a short tour of the main floor, she took me upstairs to my office on the third floor, which I shared with three other senators, one being Senator Joe Welsh, a Democrat from Dubuque. After 1985, Senator James Riordan, a Democrat from Waukee, shared the office with me. At the time, I had one staffer who served as my secretary. As we walked through the space, I noticed there was a typewriter and a small desk for the secretary to use.

Secretary Thayer did not introduce me to other senators during the tour. Instead, we just kind of introduced ourselves to each other as we met throughout the day. She explained that in addition to my staff and the staff of the other three senators, the Democratic Caucus and Republican Caucus also housed their staff on the third floor of the capitol. The caucus staff conducted extensive research and supported their respective caucuses, and it was exciting to be working in such close proximity to them. They had free access to the senate floor, where I spent most of my time. During my tenure, the caucuses assisted senators with background information about particular bills and were invaluable.

After seeing my office, Secretary Thayer showed me the desk that had been assigned to me on the floor of the senate. I took a moment to take it all in, noticing the other desks on the senate floor and imagining what it would be like to hold hearings in the meeting rooms and to debate on the senate floor soon after. Little did I know then that I would end up spending most of my time at that desk on the senate floor.

Secretaries also sat on the senate floor with their respective senators. Senators generally relied on the caucus staff and the Legislative Services Bureau for their research. I would also soon learn that the capitol was very cramped for space. Whenever senators had meetings with constituents and lobbyists, we would often use the senate's cloakroom or the rotunda of the capitol. We normally stood and talked during these meetings but could also sit in the senate's lounge when meetings ran longer. While I was there, legislators often talked about moving the Supreme Court out of the capitol. However, this did not happen until years after I had left and the legislature built a new building for the high court.

While somewhat crowded for office space, the state capitol is a beautiful building with a gold dome on top that many Americans have probably seen on television during the Iowa caucuses where the first major presidential caucuses are held. And from January of 1983 to January of 1990, it was my home away from home. In addition to the senate chamber and the high court, the capitol also housed the chambers of the house as well as the main office for the attorney general, a grand state law library, and the offices of the secretary of state and state treasurer.

Committee Assignments

Overall, I found the state senate to be very welcoming and cordial. I was overcome by how willing everyone was to lend a helping hand, Democrat and Republican alike. While I wasn't nervous to be starting my work at the senate, I was feeling a little uncertain. Since this was new terrain for me, I wanted to avoid making any rookie mistakes. To get more rooted in my role, I sought advice from Democratic Senators Doyle, Carr, and Slater. Some of the things I asked them included the protocol on the timing of first speeches, how to file amendments, where to file bills, and what the general process was for passing legislation. I had a great working relationship with them and appreciated how I could rely on them for solid counsel on matters like these.

Just prior to beginning my first legislative session, I had received a notice letter from Senator Lowell Junkins, a Democrat from Montrose and the Majority Leader in the senate, outlining my committee assignments. Committee assignments lasted for two years, and I worked on a variety of legislative matters during the two-year assignments. I was pleased to learn that I had been appointed to serve as the vice-chair of the Judiciary Committee, which was chaired by Senator Donald Doyle, a Democrat from Sioux City. I also was appointed to be a member of the Human Resources Committee, chaired by Senator Robert Carr, a Democrat from Dubuque. I was also appointed to be a member of the Local Government Committee, chaired by Senator Alvin Miller, a Democrat from Ventura, and a member of the Small Business and Economic Development Committee, chaired by Senator Emil Husak, a Democrat from Tama. I was also appointed to serve on the Senate Appropriations Committee on Corrections and Mental Health, which was chaired by Senator Carr.

I soon learned that the committee meeting rooms were located in the back of the house and senate chambers. As a freshman senator, my good friend Senator Doyle gave me much responsibility on the Judiciary Committee. As vice-chair, I was the workhorse of the committee. I worked on all manner of bills and received eighty-five to ninety percent support from my fellow Democrats. I also offered many amendments. As with all bills, some passed and others didn't.

In my new role, I handled the large majority of the bills that came through the Judiciary Committee. As such, I had exclusive control over the life and death of those bills, as any bill that did not report out of subcommittee would die and not have a chance to become law. Bills killed by a subcommittee chair are simply assigned to the subcommittee until the end of the session, with a new session beginning every two years. If a senator wanted to revive a "dead" bill, they would have an opportunity to do so at the beginning of the new session.

In addition to my service on the Judiciary Committee, I was very pleased to serve on the Appropriations Committee for Corrections and Mental Health. During my tenure as an assistant attorney general, I had represented the mental health and corrections agencies, so I was a logical fit. Whenever issues affecting the prison system came before the committee, Senator Carr would rely on Senator Doyle and me to share our opinions before he cast his vote.

For the 1984–85 term, Senator Junkins reappointed me to serve as vice-chair of the Judiciary Committee, which was still chaired by Senator Doyle. I was also appointed to the State Government Committee, chaired by Senator Carr, and I continued to serve on the Local Government Committee, which was chaired by Senator Miller. In addition, I was appointed to the Labor and Business Relations Committee, chaired by Senator Joe Welsh. I appreciated my new assignments and felt that I must be doing well if I was allowed to remain on the committees and had been assigned to some new ones so early in my first term.

Senator Milo Colton, a Democrat from Sioux City, and I offered a full employment bill in 1983 that did not survive. But I had run for the senate on a promise of full employment, so I sought to fulfill that promise. Senator Doyle, Senator Colton, and I were inseparable and would often go to lunch together. The three of us also went to many of the same legislative functions at night. On occasion, we were invited to separate lunches, but we tried to stick together whenever we could. We each drove a blue Cadillac, which was sheer coincidence. I bought my 1968 car from Senator Lee Holt, a Republican from Spencer, who owned a car dealership. Senator Holt chose the car for me and drove it from the dealership to the capitol. Senator Doyle already owned his car, and Senator Colton bought his later. The three of us also commiserated about the failure to enact certain bills, such as the full employment bill, until Senator Colton lost the 1985 election. I was surprised and disappointed to learn that he would not continue to serve in the senate. I had thought Senator Colton and I would work together for many years. I remained close with Senator Doyle over the years. Leala and I would have him over to the house for dinner on occasion. And when he passed in 2007, I drove the fourteen hours from Austin to attend his funeral in Sioux City.

During the legislative session that began in 1985, I decided to follow in Senator Doyle's footsteps and hire a court reporter to be my secretary. Lori Bristol was a great secretary and went on to become the secretary of the senate in 1990. She was an efficient and invaluable employee. As a court reporter, Lori's skills included taking down committee debates verbatim. This was important for the standing committees that I chaired (Labor and Ethics), as I often had to go back and review what each senator had said.

In 1985 and 1986, I received my new committee assignments from Senator Junkins. He had appointed me to serve as the chair of the Labor and Industrial Relations Committee. For the next two years, I would also serve as vice-chair of the Judiciary Committee, chaired by Senator

Doyle, and be a member of the State Government Committee, chaired by Senator Carr, as well as a member of the Appropriations Committee on State Government, chaired by Senator Pat Deluhery, a Democrat from Davenport.

In 1987, I received my new committee assignments from Senator C. W. "Bill" Hutchins, a Democrat from Audubon, who was the new Majority Leader in the senate. I began to look forward to these assignments and was happy to learn that I'd been appointed to serve as the chair of the Ethics Committee. During that time, I would also serve as vice-chair of the Judiciary Committee, chaired by Senator Doyle; a member of the Business and Labor Relations Committee, chaired by Senator James Wells, a Democrat from Cedar Rapids; a member of the Commerce Committee, chaired by Senator William Palmer, a Democrat from Des Moines; and a member of the Justice System Appropriations Committee, chaired by Senator Gene Fraise who was a Democrat from Fort Madison.

I was admitted to the United States Supreme Court in September of 1987 by motion. Brent Appel, Iowa Assistant Attorney General, made the motion to admit me to practice before the court. I was sponsored on the recommendations of Attorney General Thomas J. Miller and Iowa Assistant Attorney General Stephen C. Robinson.

In 1989, Majority Leader Hutchins issued my new two-year committee assignments. I was happy to learn that I had been appointed to serve as President Pro Tempore of the senate. This was a great honor, and I took the responsibility seriously. I thoroughly enjoyed presiding over the senate where I ruled on motions, points of order, and other parliamentary matters and kept order. I knew the senate's rule book well and felt this was a natural fit for me. Lieutenant Governor Jo Ann Zimmerman was president of the senate and second in line to be governor. As President Pro Tempore, I was third in line to be governor and presided over the senate in Lieutenant Governor Zimmerman's absence.

I would also serve as a member of the Judiciary Committee, chaired by Senator Doyle, and be a member of the Administration Committee, which was chaired by Senator Michael Gronstal, a Democrat from Council Bluffs. Other assignments included serving as a member of the Business and Labor Relations Committee, chaired by Senator John Petersen, a Democrat from Albia, and serving on the Commerce Committee, chaired by Senator Palmer.

Private Practice

Leala and Linda continued to operate their law practice while I served in the legislature. After my first legislative session was over, Leala and Linda moved their practice to an office on Douglas Avenue in Des Moines. Leala and Linda continued to work as partners, and I worked solo. It was a nice office. I remember the front door opened to a small receptionist area with two desks and chairs. Leala and Linda had also hired Lana Wycoff as their secretary so they could have help handling administrative matters in the office. The law office was about three miles from our home on Lower Beaver Road, which was very convenient. I had a large single office in the front of the building, and Leala and Linda had nice large offices in the rear. There also was a conference room where we met with our clients.

In the new office, Leala worked wills and trusts, bankruptcy, and anything that fell under general practice. Linda worked cases dealing with employment law, civil rights, and general practice. And I worked employment law/civil rights. Leala and Linda operated as Pettit and Mann; whereas, I operated as Thomas Mann, Jr., Attorney at Law.

Cases

In April of 1988, I took over one civil rights case from Linda that was prosecuted against the City of Redfield in Iowa. During that case, I successfully persuaded a jury to award my client $65,000 for age discrimination and wrongful discharge. Unfortunately, that case was reversed on appeal.

In April of 1989, I took on a case of racial discrimination. As a result of my efforts to defend Police Cadet Charlie Smith and Terry Kemp, the Des Moines City Council voted to pay two cadets $32,000 total after they complained of racist behavior in the police department. Charlie Smith and Terry Kemp were Des Moines Police Cadets falsely accused of lying about hearing a supervising officer use the N-word.

This case was tried before the Des Moines Civil Service Commission. It displayed the "cop code," which is a code cops use to support each other by lying under oath. Fortunately, we were able to prevail, and the case was settled in Ms. Smith's and Mr. Kemp's favor.

At the time of the hearing, I had just supported and passed legislation in the senate limiting the use of lie detector tests as evidence in court. To this day, lie detectors are still not considered one hundred percent reliable. Charlie Smith took a lie detector test to prove her innocence. Ironically, we could not use the results of her test because of the legislation I had authored. As the Des Moines Register suggested, I was "hoisted on my own petard."

Despite this, Charlie Smith was given her job back. She was fired after filing a complaint against the department about racist behavior, and the money was divided between Ms. Smith, another cadet (Terry Kemp), and me. In exchange for the payout, Smith dropped her suit against the department.

During this time, the ICRC won a sex bias case against the Des Moines Police Department, seven years after the initial complaint. The ICRC found that Myrle Atwood was discriminated against when she was not allowed to perform light duty at regular pay while she was pregnant. She was the first female police officer to become pregnant and was treated differently than the male officers in that she had to perform regular duty for regular pay.

While the Myrle Atwood case was not my case, the Atwood case and the Deborah Lynch case—a case that was prosecuted by my friend and mentor, feminist, and first Iowa female gubernatorial candidate, Roxanne Conlin, a Democrat from Des Moines—along with the Charlie Smith case that I won, helped remove barriers for women in the Des Moines Police Department, when women were just getting a toe hold.

Roxanne and I had worked together in the Attorney General's Office. She was representing the ICRC, and I worked with her on several cases during my tenure there. I remember Roxanne as a very skilled and capable attorney. I also handled Marlon Williams' case against the Central Iowa job training agency. Williams was wrongfully discharged from the agency and sought my counsel. We were successful and brought suit, obtaining a settlement of $72,500.

Double Duty

I worked private cases concurrently with the legislative sessions, which was starting to take a toll on my health. The stress was giving me an ulcer, and Leala and I discussed off and on whether I should seek a second senate term. Ultimately, I decided to run again because I was enjoying the work at the state legislature. To help matters, I took fewer cases between January and May of the year, which was the general time for the legislative session.

However, some of my cases had longer lives, as it took time to draft the pleadings, do discovery, and eventually go to trial, so there was still some work that I needed to address while in session. For example, a case that started in June (my time off from the legislature) might still be lingering in

February or March of the following year while I was in session. And since the courts set scheduling deadlines for cases, I was forced to devote some time to the practice during legislative session.

Except for time taken for illness and to try a few cases in Waterloo during the 1989 and 1990 sessions, I generally had a good attendance record at the legislature. I would go to the capitol around 8:30 a.m. when we were in session. Committee meetings started around 9:00 a.m. and continued through the day. Legislative floor work might be in the afternoon until around 5:00 p.m., depending on the day. After that, there were legislative functions to attend, such as meetings sponsored by the Chamber of Commerce or other groups interested in legislative actions. I would attend the lobbying meetings that were pertinent to legislation I was working on. And around 9:30 p.m., if I had not gone home at 5:00 p.m., I left the legislative functions and went to the law office and checked the mail and any pleadings that may have come in during the day. After that, I went home, which often made for a long day.

Key Legislation

South African Divestiture

I worked on many pieces of significant legislation during my service in the Iowa state legislature. The most memorable perhaps was the South African divestiture legislation that I began during my first senate term. I was committed to the divestiture bill because it was the right thing to do. I had been educated about the mistreatment of blacks in South Africa by young activists working in the legislature. In 1983, I went to New York City to participate in a debate the United Nations was having about South Africa and the divestiture movement taking place all across the world.

Apartheid was a subject that I was all too familiar with growing up in the Jim Crow South where schools and public spaces were legally segregated with signs posted, labeled "White" and "Colored," hung by oppressors, lest minorities forget their place in society. When I saw an opportunity to work on this bill, I took up a leadership role that would force the State of Iowa to divest any funds it had invested in companies that were doing business in South Africa.

Initially, the South African divesture bill was opposed by Democrats and Republicans alike. Senator Charles Miller, a Democrat from Burlington, kept the bill bottled up in committee during our initial efforts to move it. When the redrafted bill got assigned to Senator Berl Priebe, a Democrat from Algona, during the next legislative session, I cut a deal with him by agreeing to support a farm bill of his that would cut taxes for farmers, and the bill moved out of the State Government Committee. However, Senator Jack Nystrom, a Republican from Boone, opposed the bill on the floor.

In spite of opposition from both sides of the aisle, on April 9th, 1984, the Iowa senate passed my bill to impose restrictions on South Africa. My bill would require the withdrawal of more than 100 million dollars of state investments in American companies that did business with South Africa and supported Apartheid. I felt it was wrong to use state dollars to prop up a racist regime, and fortunately the majority of the senate and house did, too. Unfortunately, Governor Branstad vetoed the bill later that year.

I always thought that my bill was only lukewarmly supported by Majority Leader Lowell Junkins. I felt that Senator Junkins and Minority Leader, Senator Calvin Hultman, a Republican from Red Oak, conspired to keep the bill bottled up in committee. While I can't prove it, it was just one of those feelings you get whenever you have cause to watch out for people. When Senator Junkins called the bill up for debate, I noticed that he and Senator Hultman exchanged a knowing look. Immediately after, Senator Hultman was up on the floor, opposing the bill, which meant that most Republicans would oppose it. Over time, I learned how the legislative game was played and adjusted my approach accordingly.

Unfortunately, I could not persuade Senator Miller to move this bill. I killed many more bills than Senator Miller did, however, so it was not anything personal. When the divestiture bill did not make it out of committee in 1983, I simply called up to the Legislative Services Bureau in 1985 and asked that the divestiture bill be drafted for introduction into the 1985 legislative session. I would not have benefitted from redrafting the bill in 1983, as it would have been assigned again to the State Government Committee and the same subcommittee with Senator Miller as chair.

The governor, and many others, opposed the bill because of its potential economic impact on Iowa. They supported open economic commerce at any cost. In 1985 the bill was again considered and introduced to a different subcommittee chaired by Senator Berl Priebe of Kossuth. I cut a deal. When the bill was debated on the floor, Senator Arthur Small, a Democrat from Iowa City offered an amendment that was adopted. The amendment modified the bill to ban investment in companies that had not agreed to sign onto the "Sullivan Principles." The Sullivan Principles required companies to agree to pay and treat all their employees equally. Approximately one-hundred-and-twenty companies had signed the Sullivan Principles, which made the bill more palatable to the governor.

I'm happy to report that in March of 1985, the senate and house passed the South Africa divestiture bill. And this time Governor Branstad approved the bill, much to the chagrin of Senator Jack Nystrom who still opposed the bill and hoped the governor would veto it like he did the year prior. Nystrom stated he had always been against the bill, saying we shouldn't conduct foreign policy in the state senate and that he didn't think the bill would help blacks anyway.

It seems that Senator Nystrom did not fully understand the situation. South Africa was the only country in the world that mandated racial discrimination by law. Blacks made up seventy-five percent of the population but had no voice in their own government. They paid higher taxes but weren't given a proper education. In short, they were subjected to an apartheid policy and by supporting companies that supported apartheid, we were, in fact, hurting blacks.

Perhaps I make the passing of this legislation sound easy or matter of fact, but it was anything but. As a black man who was taught from an early age to be subservient to white people, particularly those in positions of authority, this bill was starting to take a toll on my health. I was beginning to show signs of anxiety. I was sweating through my suit jackets in committee meetings as I anticipated having to speak out again about the legislation that was so important to me to pass. It took effort and a few tries and years to convince others to sign onto it. Some games were played, too, such as the time I was left out of a meeting about the divestiture bill when an official from South Africa (Johann Groebler) came to visit.

I wasn't disappointed or rattled about not being invited to the meeting with the other legislators. I was the prime sponsor of the divestiture bill, and Groebler wasn't going to convince me to change my mind. I did, however, express surprise to the press when I was interviewed for an article in the local paper, as a means of criticizing Groebler's actions. Groebler was being sneaky, and my being excluded from the meeting was akin to the Baker's Square situation where, as a state senator, I was overlooked when standing in line in a restaurant in Des Moines to purchase a pie while several white patrons, who arrived after me, were served ahead of me. I objected to the situation and when management did nothing to rectify the situation, I walked out and took my business elsewhere. Being "invisible" or excluded based on the color of my skin was a familiar yet unsettling experience for me.

Pay for College Athletes

In 1987, I filed a bill to create pay for college athletes. I argued that many colleges were simply exploiting their student athletes by bringing them to campus and placing more emphasis on athletics than academics. I argued that only a minority of college athletes go on to play professional sports and that colleges ought not to be in the business of teaching, fostering, or permitting corruption to exist. Unfortunately, the bill did not pass, and college athletics are still facing this problem today.

Factory Lockouts

On March 19th, 1987, the Iowa Senate approved a Benefits bill, affecting workers who have been idle because of factory lockouts. With this new bill, which was supported by the Business and Labor Committee, factory workers could now collect unemployment benefits whenever a factory shut down, which is different than a strike when a laborer ceases working to protest a dispute. Twenty-two other states had similar rules, and I was growing tired of hearing Republicans accuse any measure that helps workers as being anti-business.

In my opinion, this argument by the Republicans was a red herring, a shibboleth, and had nothing to do with anti-business. Instead, it had to do with representing the best interests of all state workers. Senator Calvin Hultman and other Republican senators claimed it was a labor dispute and did not agree with me. Fortunately, the bill passed the senate and the house anyway. As we were working on the bill, Governor Branstad cautioned that it may be unconstitutional and that he was opposed to it. The governor said the bill would create a negative business climate, but he did not end up vetoing it after it passed the senate and house.

The bill passed into law later that year. The most opposition that I faced in the senate came from Republicans. Because the Democrats were in the majority in both the house and senate, eighty-five to ninety percent of the time, I had my way with most issues. There was some occasional opposition from Democrats, like with the South African divestiture bill. But, in general, if I was able to get a bill out of committee, I received Democrat support on the floor, which meant passage.

Gun Control

In 1987, I took a shot at gun control legislation when a bill was introduced to prevent communities from passing local gun laws that were more restrictive than state laws. I opposed the bill because there were already too many guns in this country and the state laws were contradictory to the home-rule status given to local communities by the legislature. Under home rule, communities were to govern themselves. I also opposed it because there are too many guns in this country. The bill passed the senate, but it died in the house, so it did not have a chance to become law.

Handicapped Rights

In February of 1989, I was also an advocate for the handicapped. In 1988, I shepherded a study bill that provided that deaf jurors would be given a sign language interpreter at the taxpayer's expense. This bill gave to deaf jurors the right to serve on juries the same as any other citizen. It was a matter of citizenship and equity to pass this bill. The bill was approved by the Judiciary Committee without dissent and became a statewide law.

Wiretapping

In 1989, Governor Brandstad introduced a study bill that permitted state police agencies to use phone wiretapping in certain criminal cases with a judge's approval. Efforts to pass wiretapping legislation had gone on for about twenty years prior. During my time in the legislature, previous wiretapping study bills had been assigned to my subcommittee and killed. I killed them because Senator Doyle and I generally agreed that wiretapping legislation was an invasion of privacy. In 1989, however, law enforcement and the governor's office finally submitted a study bill that contained many new and good due process protections. On reading that bill, I decided to move it out of committee. It was not clear how long I would continue to serve in the legislature, and I reasoned that, sooner or later, wiretapping would be passed. I decided that if it was going to become law, it should contain good due process protections for citizens. The bill, which was signed into law, contained adequate safeguards, including a judge's supervision of wiretaps and a guarantee that citizens could seek civil damages if the eavesdropping proved to be unjustified.

Hate Crimes

On February 9th, 1990, the senate passed a unanimous bill that would prevent violence against certain groups by prohibiting hate crimes, such as cross burning and harassment of homosexuals. The new bill would also increase penalties for these and other hate crimes. The hate crimes bill was introduced as a study bill. Study bills were anonymous. They did not have the clear fingerprints of a particular house member or senator on them.

This bill took the moral high ground in the sense that it did not condemn, nor condone, racism or homosexuality. Instead, it spoke to whether or not it was justified to allow people to be beaten or abused based on the color of their skin or their sexual orientation. The hate crimes bill was assigned to the Judiciary Committee and to a subcommittee chaired by me. I moved the bill out of subcommittee and through the Judiciary Committee. On the senate floor, the bill was managed by Senator Richard Varn, a Democrat from Solon. In March of that year, a hate crimes measure was sent to the governor, and the bill became law. This law would allow a felony prison sentence of up to two years for anyone who maliciously intimidated another person based on race, religion, age, disability, or sexual orientation.

Economic Development

On March 28th, 1986, an article in *The Des Moines Register* addressed the lack of business opportunity for African Americans in the state of Iowa. One of my campaign promises was to create more business opportunities for minority constituents. To work on fulfilling this promise, Senator Colton and I had introduced a full-employment economic development bill in 1983. Unfortunately, the bill did not become law at that time.

In 1986, I persuaded Senator Joe Welsh to insert some economic development language for blighted communities in Des Moines and Waterloo into the budget bill, which made it more palatable to the other senators. The full employment bill died, but the economic development language passed. This portion of the bill then passed in the house and was signed into law by the governor that year.

Due Process

Overall, I worked well with all of the state senators. Compromise, however, was difficult to come by. As stated earlier, Democrats were in control in the senate and the house, and depending on the bill, they would compromise with Republicans. During my tenure, I sponsored a bill with Senator Ray Taylor, a Republican from Steamboat Rock. The bill dealt with constitutional due process protections. I wanted to define and make sure that due process protections would last and be interpreted by the courts in the manner that I thought proper. Senator Taylor took a lot of heat from others in his party for being on the bill and had to back away from his support because of how I was defining the issue. As a result, the bill died, and I did not try to revive it.

Family Life

When working in the state legislature, I worked long hours but managed to spend time with Leala and Nari at night and on weekends. I still read to Nari on weekends, which was something we both treasured. At the end of the legislative session in 1983, Leala, Nari, Uncle Al, Aunt Barbara, and my mom, Flossie, took a trip to Winnipeg, Canada. Uncle Al and Aunt Barb lived in St. Paul, Minnesota. For the trip, Uncle Al rented a Ford van and drove down to Des Moines for a visit. We then piled into the van and drove to St. Paul, Minnesota. From there we drove to Fargo, North Dakota, and on to Winnipeg. We toured Winnipeg and took a boat trip while we were there. On the boat, I danced with Leala, my mom, and Nari. We all had a great time. Even the road trip was fun. To help pass the time in the car, we played various games, pairing off into teams. Nari, in particular, had great fun and loved the games. Sometimes Nari and I teamed together. Other times, Nari and Aunt Barb teamed together. It was a long drive, so we would switch back and forth. Most of the games dealt with trivia. Nari and Barb were pretty good at them. And sometimes as we drove, we tried to guess what states the license plates on the next car would be from. Nari always delighted whenever we guessed correctly.

Kari

A few years into my first senate term, Leala became pregnant with our second child. Leala and I both wanted to have more children, so we were delighted to learn that our family was growing. Leala took prenatal vitamins, and the best that I can recall she had a normal pregnancy without any complications. In July 1985, our second daughter Kari was born. We named her after my grandmother Carrie Maclin, after Leala agreed to an alternate spelling.

Fortunately, it was not a difficult birth for Leala, as had been the case with Nari. We took some photos in the delivery room once Kari had arrived. Nari, Leala's brother George, and I were present for the birth. George's girlfriend, Karen, was also there with us. I was proud to be a father, twice over.

Kari was a quiet baby and grew into a shy baby girl. She would prepare to cry at the least scolding. Nari loved her new sister and insisted on holding her on her lap often. After Kari's birth, Leala would occasionally stop by the capitol with Nari and Kari. A few months before Kari was born, Leala and Linda had separated as law partners. Soon after, Leala and I began working as Mann and Mann at our office on Douglas Avenue in Des Moines. I would take both girls to the law office on Saturday mornings so that I could spend more time with them.

Both Nari and Kari attended public schools. They were sent to Woodlawn School, which was about a block away from our house. Although they were daughters of a state legislator, they were treated like all the other children attending public school. On occasion, Nari's teacher would invite me to come speak to her class, and I would stop by Nari's school to talk about my favorite books and author John Le Carrè. I soon found out that the espionage written about in Le Carrè's books was too heavy a subject for grade schoolers, so I also answered questions from students about my daily activities as a senator. I told them about committee meetings and debates on the senate floor and what it was like to attend legislative functions. Other parents were invited to speak on occasion, and Nari would come home and share what she had learned from them.

Since we decided we would place our girls in daycare, Leala continued to work full-time. However, she did take some leave for Kari's birth and to spend time with her at home afterward. When Kari was born, I did not take any leave from the law practice, and since the birth occurred after the legislative session, I did not need to take any leave from the senate.

Kari is a kind and gentle person. Like Nari, Kari grew into a studious kid. She finished high school at the Texas Academy of Math and Science in Denton, Texas. She got her undergraduate degree in psychology at the University of Southern California, Los Angeles. She then obtained a master's degree in sports psychology from Texas Christian University in Fort Worth. Afterward, she received a doctorate in physical therapy after studying at Texas State University in San Marcos. She now works as a physical therapist in Austin, Texas.

A Second Term

While I was busy, at the time I did not reflect too much on the stress of being an attorney and a legislator. Both had been my life's goals, and it was marvelous to have achieved both. But I didn't dwell on it much because I didn't want my success to go to my head. I was ambitious before I ever got to the senate. I knew that I was going to run for higher office whenever the opportunity presented itself. Unfortunately, I couldn't run for U.S. Congress at the time, because popular Democratic Congressman Neal Smith was my congressman, and I couldn't run for the U.S. Senate because popular Democratic Senator Tom Harkin occupied that seat. I had to wait my turn.

So, in 1985, I started my run for a second term in the state senate. I ran unopposed in the primary and the general election. Looking back, I ran a good campaign. I campaigned as I had done previously, perhaps not as hard, since I didn't have any negative tactics thrown at me like I had when Trucano was running for the state seat. I do recall doing some canvassing, posting yard signs, and making public appearances along with a few guest radio spots. My intent to run for a second term also appeared in the local papers.

While it was still nerve-wracking awaiting the returns on election night this time around, Leala says she noticed I had a quiet confidence about me that evening. She says she picked up on it and had a feeling that I would keep my seat.

Chapter 9

A Role Model

...[A] role model in the flesh provides more than inspiration; his or her very existence is confirmation of possibilities one may have every reason to doubt, saying yes, someone like me can do this.
— *Supreme Court Justice Sonya Sotomayor*

Governor Branstad

While in office, I considered carefully my actions and influence as a public role model. I wanted to do everything that I could to set a positive example for others not only in my work as a legislator, but also as a public speaker and public official of good standing. During Governor Branstad's inaugural address in 1983, I was impressed, albeit surprised, when he touched on "meeting human needs," as this was something I also strove for. I interpreted that statement as an olive branch to the Democrats in both houses of legislature who had called for cooperation between parties. Unfortunately, the branch didn't make it to the legislature.

It soon became clear that Governor Branstad did not share the same values as the Democrats, as he failed to show the same level of compassion for human needs. Democrats found it difficult to work with Republicans under his administration. In fact, we had to sue Governor Branstad over his use of the item veto. Branstad was not generally supportive of my work. He was conservative, and I was one of the most liberal senators in the state senate. We did not often see eye-to-eye.

On June 9th, 1987, Governor Branstad was presented a bill that would give rights to handicapped citizens. The bill would have, consistent with the federal requirements, required an employer to reasonably accommodate the disabled by supplying a reader if the disabled person was blind and the job included paperwork; supplying an interpreter if the disabled person was deaf and the job required telephone contact; supplying adequate workspace and access to it if the disabled person used a wheelchair; and providing minor adjustments in working hours if the disabled person was required to visit a clinic or rehabilitation center for treatment. Unfortunately, Branstad vetoed this bill and, to my knowledge, was the first governor in Iowa to veto any civil rights legislation.

Certificates

During my time in the state senate, I received various certificates and awards for my public service. I served on the Board of Directors for the Central Iowa Chapter of the American Red Cross from July of 1977 to June of 1983. For six years, I assisted the Red Cross by attending board meetings and working to make policies for the board and staff.

I was also given an award by the Regional Executive Council on Civil Rights (RECCR) on November 17th, 1983, an organization that I helped establish. I trained RECCR members, including the civil rights investigators and commissioners. It was a pleasure to do so. While serving as the director of the ICRC, I gave presentations to commissioners and staff of civil rights agencies in Iowa, Nebraska, Missouri, and Kansas. I lectured on civil rights laws and issues and also did so after being elected senator.

In 1985, I was given an award for general services to the community. This award was given by Latonya Ward and Jerry

Daniels. The award reflected my participation in various community activities, such as the NAACP, the AFL-CIO, and KUCB's Community Radio Program. I also received a KUCB award the following year, which was given to me by Joanna Cheatom. I supported KUCB, and KUCB supported my political campaigns.

Labor unions have been the means by which workers have joined together to obtain better wages, benefits, and working conditions. I believe in labor unions and became a union member after my legislative service. In 1987, the AFL-CIO awarded me the AFL-CIO Community Services Counseling Programs award for stimulating and training union members to help their fellow workers, families, and citizens live a better life in a more representative and responsive community. I was pleased to receive this award, which was given to me by AFL-CIO Des Moines chapter president, Perry Chapin.

Speeches

Civil Rights

As a state senator, I was occasionally asked to give speeches at special events. In a speech that I gave to students at Perry Community High School on Martin Luther King, Jr.'s birthday on January 19th, 1989, I spoke about civil rights to inspire these students to take action in the community and to make a difference. Because of Dr. King and other civil rights leaders, I was able to attend college, become a lawyer, an assistant attorney general, and a state senator. In turn, I wanted to inspire students so they would continue with their education and have more opportunities later in life, just as I had.

In my speech I reminded them, "The revolution is not over. There has been progress and change, but it is not done." In my opinion, there has been much change in race and gender relations in this nation over the past seventy-five years. Blacks are able to vote and no longer face the "Whites Only" signs prevalent during the Jim Crow era, and women are treated with more equity than they were prior to being given the right to vote in 1920. But things are not perfect for blacks or for women. There has been progress and change, but, as I said in my speech, much work remains to be done.

I gave a version of this speech on the senate floor on January 15th, 1985, to honor Dr. King. It was an opportunity for me to remind myself and to ask others to rededicate themselves to the task of achieving Dr. King's dream. It was an opportunity to ask the community to build a lasting monument to Dr. King's memory by resolving to work to accomplish the goals that he gave his life for. I concluded my speech with a plea to all in attendance, "And like a tree, let our commitment take root, and survive, and grow, and produce the fruits of justice, equality, peace, and freedom for all Iowans, all Americans, and indeed, all humankind."

Political Activism

On occasion, I was asked to give commencement speeches. I remember one that I gave on May 22nd, 1983. I crafted my words to encourage students to take action in their own communities. The way I saw it, speeches were my way of trying to educate the public about the issues of the day. It was also an opportunity for me to encourage people to become active participants in their communities. As a political figure, I was looked up to, and I was particularly desirous of encouraging young graduates to take part in community activities. As I told the students, borrowing from Henry Wadsworth Longfellow, "We judge ourselves by what we feel capable of doing; others judge us by what we have done."

In 1990, I spoke to the Big 8 Conference on Black Student Government. I reminded the students that they were the future and that they were going to be best prepared to resolve the problems facing this nation. I told the students that I co-chaired Jesse Jackson's Iowa Campaign in 1988. During my speech I spoke of standing on the floor of the Democratic National Convention in Atlanta, Georgia. I shared with them how I stood there on the convention floor listening to Jesse speak. And how as I stood there, I recognized the historical importance of the Jackson campaign. I recognized for the first time that a black man had been taken seriously as a candidate for the highest office in this land. I knew that it had been done grudgingly, but it had been done.

I knew that in the early days, the media wrote Jesse off as just a potential "power broker" at the convention, stating that he had no chance of winning the nomination. And I knew that his power broker status had begun to change when Jesse won double-digit voter support in states with small minority populations—states like Iowa with a small black population of about 1.9%. It continued when Jesse consistently won between twenty and thirty percent of the vote in all midwestern states—states essentially devoid of black populations. Soon after, he won five southern states on Super Tuesday and came in second in just about all of the others. And when he won, outright, the state of Michigan, with fifty-five percent of the vote, the change had occurred. Jesse Jackson was suddenly taken seriously as a candidate for president.

I knew that this was a historic moment for black people. Jesse Jackson had broken the color barrier, and a significant number of white voters had sent a message that they would ignore the color of a candidate's skin and vote for the candidate that best expressed their hopes, their dreams, and their aspirations. I knew that Jackson's candidacy had turned a corner for black people. Jesse had opened a door, and someday a black person would walk through that door. In

2008, it would be Barack Obama who would accomplish that.

When speaking to the students, I was pleased to see that they participated in their student government. I spoke of my prior involvement in student government and my election to the senate. I told them that I took no pride in the fact that I was the first black senator in Iowa in over 136 years. I did, however, let them know that I took pride in my personal achievement. Pride in the fact that I was able to work with various constituencies and to convince them to maintain an awareness and sensitivity to the economic, political, and social needs of the poor, disadvantaged, and minority citizens of the state and the nation.

During my speeches, I asked the students to develop a social conscience. I told them that my generation would not solve the problem of economic racial injustice and that they would inherit this problem of social injustice. It was my contention that every citizen owes a duty to the community in which they live. And this duty requires that those of us who care about preserving the rights and human dignity of all persons develop long-term strategies for bringing about change. People must either write, speak, or act. Any and all of these strategies are legitimate weapons. No greater responsibility for doing so exists than for those who have been trained for the future.

For the poor and disadvantaged, education often offers the only opportunity for upward mobility within this society. In a message to Congress on January 11th, 1962, President John F. Kennedy stated that "[a] child miseducated is a child lost." I have to agree with him, for without a good education, it is difficult to find a good job. And without a good job, it is difficult to take care of yourself and your family because you will struggle with the basics, such as buying clothing, food, shelter, and reliable transportation.

Voter Suppression

I gave another speech on February 4th, 1984. During this speech, I spoke to the new branch of the NAACP at Fort Dodge. I spoke about the voter suppression tactics toward minorities, which is still a problem today. Speaking to the Fort Dodge branch of the NAACP gave me a chance to remind the community that, while many legal impediments to voting had been removed, a substantial number of black voters were still prevented from exercising their right to vote because of irregularities, including late openings of voting places, inoperative voting machines, and incorrect delivery of voting machines to predominantly black polling places. I was inspired to see so many in attendance and hoped they would take what they heard that evening and use it as an impetus to address these issues in their community.

Discretion in the Justice System

A high proportion of inmates are black, but they are not getting a jury of their peers. During some of my speeches, I spoke to the issue of too much discretion in the justice system: discretion in the prosecutor's role in charging crimes, discretion in the judge's role in ruling on the admissibility of evidence, and discretion in juries in deciding guilt or innocence. The unfortunate result of this discretion is that the prisons are filled with blacks. I combatted this by trying to educate people on the issue. I spoke to several branches of the NAACP about this. I also served on the Senate Appropriations Committee on Corrections and Mental Health. And whenever I had philosophical disagreements with the prison administration, I expressed those disagreements directly.

South Africa Divestiture

On February 18th, 1985, I gave a speech at the YWCA during Black History Week. During the speech, I mentioned the South Africa divestiture legislation I was working on. Speaking about South Africa gave me a chance to explain why it was immoral for the state of Iowa to invest in companies that were doing business in South Africa.

South Africa was the only nation in the family of nations that mandated oppression against the majority of its people by law because of the color of their skin. In South Africa, fifteen percent of the people occupy eighty-seven percent of the land mass. At the time, South Africa had a population of approximately thirty-one million people, twenty-two million or seventy-three percent of whom were black or African, four million or fifteen percent were white, and approximately three million or eleven percent were classified as colored or of mixed races.

I shared how in South Africa, the whites had appropriated for themselves eighty-seven percent of the land mass, including the most fertile land that contained diamonds and gold mines. Whereas, the blacks were denied their birthright to citizenship and were forcibly removed to live on thirteen percent of the land, the so-called "Homelands" or "Bantustans," what Americans might recognize as reservations. In South Africa, the government practiced a policy of apartheid, a policy of keeping the races separated, similar to the Jim Crow era we experienced here in the United States. The rights of the South African people were determined based on the racial group to which they belonged. Race determined where people were allowed to live, what work they could do, what education they could receive, and what political rights they may have, if any. In South Africa, blacks over the age of sixteen were required to carry a passbook at all times. The passbook determined whether the person could travel from one city to the next, whether the person could work, and the kind of work that the person would be permitted to do.

I also shared that in South Africa, blacks were relegated to the lower-paying, less skillful jobs. Blacks did not receive equal pay for equal work. In South Africa, black women and children remained at home on the reservations, while the men went into the mines and other allowed places of work. The families were separated for most of the year because the government was anti-family.

In South Africa, blacks were denied the right to vote and denied the right to participate in the political process in any way. Free speech did not exist, and people who spoke out against the apartheid system were subject to prosecution for treason and could be banned, imprisoned, or executed. I shared all of this with attendees during my speech, because I wanted them to understand why I was so passionate about the divestiture legislation I was working on as well as the impact it would have on blacks in South Africa.

Press Coverage

Clarence Thomas

While I was a state senator, I occasionally received coverage in the Iowa papers. In an article that ran in *The Des Moines Register*, I shared my opposition to the Clarence Thomas appointment to the Supreme Court in 1991. I did not feel that Clarence Thomas was qualified to serve on the Supreme Court, either by experience or philosophy. This is because Clarence Thomas's views betrayed the black community. In the article I stated, "His general philosophy that black people need to stop relying on government assistance, stop calling for affirmative action and be people of self-reliance and pull themselves up by their bootstraps is flawed. ... You can't live with three hundred years of legalized slavery, legalized segregation, then de facto segregation, and be a vital part of the community without being self-reliant."

Voting Rights

In an October 14th, 1990, article in the Fort Dodge *Messenger*, I stated, "We don't have the luxury of calling voting a privilege. The sacrifices made [by others to obtain this right] make it an obligation." I said this, because I firmly believe that voting is not a privilege; it is an obligation. In the 1960s, many struggles were fought to ensure blacks the right to vote. In June of 1963, civil rights activist Medgar Evers was slain. On April 4th, 1968, Martin Luther King, Jr. was assassinated. And Congressman John Lewis and many others were beaten after crossing the Edmond Pettis Bridge during the Selma-to-Montgomery March in 1965 to demonstrate the desire of African Americans to exercise their constitutional right to vote.

The Voting Rights Act was adopted in 1965. Although many legal impediments to the right to vote have been removed, blacks and other minorities are still blocked from voting by way of various voter suppression tactics. We saw this in Georgia and North Dakota during the 2018 election. And we saw the Texas Secretary of State issue a false notice in 2019 that over 10,000 voters were illegal voters in Texas.

We have inherited the legacy of the martyrs of the civil rights movement of the 1960s, and the slaves before them. It was for us that Medgar Evers, Dr. Martin Luther King, and many others gave their lives. It was for us that many people suffered the slings and arrows of misfortune— people who withstood the blows of the billy clubs, the water hoses, the police dogs, and the indignity of being jailed. It was for us that people fought and died for the right to vote, and the sacrifices that they made impose upon us an obligation to vote. Because of this, we don't have the luxury of calling voting a privilege.

Ronald Reagan

In February of 1984, an article appeared in the *Sioux City Journal* citing protestors who criticized then President Ronald

Regan for being a "selfish brute." I, too, was critical of the Reagan administration, citing its policies as racist and threatening to set back the civil rights movement twenty years. I talked about how we have made progress since the days of slavery and Jim Crow and the sit-ins and civil rights demonstrations of the sixties, but I also stated that we were not where we need to be yet, as black Americans were still not on equal footing with white Americans when it came to its social, economic, and political institutions. I went on to say that the Reagan administration was hypocritical in that it publicly stated that it supported civil rights while simultaneously working to undermine them with "reverse discrimination policies," as they opposed the affirmative action plans that were in place to afford African American and minorities equal rights with education and hiring. There was also a resurgence of the KKK since Reagan had taken office.

I was of the opinion that the Reagan administration had repeatedly demonstrated its insensitivity to the plight of the majority of Americans, while at the same time pursuing that which benefited the rich and well-to-do. The evidence of Reagan administration insensitivity was shown by its policy of cutting back on social security and social welfare spending, while simultaneously serving as the prime architect of a bloated military budget. According to U.S. Census data, the Reagan policies added over two million new people to the U.S. poverty rolls, with an estimated two million who were American homeless. Just as during the Reagan administration, in the current administration, the homeless live in garages, abandoned buildings, under bridges, on park benches, and in trash dumpsters.

A Role Model for Other Minorities

It felt great to be able to help people in the state legislature. During my time there, I served as a role model for other minorities by doing my best to meet the great demands and burdens placed on me as a black elected official. I strived to be an effective spokesperson for justice and equality. I tried to make race work for black people and other minorities, and not against them. I spoke out against racism and the broad discretion within the criminal justice system. I also spoke out against the manner in which representatives were elected to school boards and city councils by at-large elections. Most of the representatives were elected at-large, thereby diluting the vote of minorities who were living in discrete districts.

Unfortunately, the problems identified with the Iowa electoral process then are still present today. The Republican Party and its members of legislatures continue to engage in voter suppression, gerrymandering, and purging voters from voter rolls. In my view, these problems require organization by voters to weed out those elected officials who do not have their best interests at heart by speaking out and exercising their constitutional right to vote in every election, be it city, state, or national.

The North may have won the shooting war, but the South won the political war. Unfortunately, the Civil War is not over. Shortly after the Civil War, Andrew Johnson was elected President. Johnson clashed with Congress over reconstruction. He vetoed legislation to protect the right of freed slaves. He opposed the rights of freed men, called for a lenient reconstruction policy, and vetoed the Freedmen's Bureau bill. This bill was meant to establish a Bureau for the Relief of Freedmen and to provide food, shelter, clothing, medical services, and land to freed slaves. Johnson was a one-term president who was impeached and acquitted by the senate.

In 1865, the KKK was established. This white hate group wreaked havoc on blacks for the next one hundred years. The KKK remains active as shown by the Unite the Right rally in Charlottesville, Virginia, in 2017. In 2019, Virginia has been embroiled in a controversy over its governor and attorney general, both having admitted to using shoe polish to appear in blackface in college. And politicians throughout the South continue to oppose the removal of monuments to Confederate soldiers, as further evidence that we are still fighting the politics of a war that should have ended over one-hundred-and-fifty years ago.

Political Activism

Anti-Apartheid Rally

On February 12th, 1990, activists gathered in Des Moines to celebrate the release of Nelson Mandela. More than one-hundred-and-fifty anti-apartheid activists gathered for this rally. I attended the rally to celebrate Mandela's release from prison. I spoke at the event and told the crowd that economic sanctions against South Africa must stay in place as the majority of South Africans remained in economic slavery.

I remember giving an interview to the TV news media during the rally as well. I shared that I was very surprised by the release of Mandela but also very pleased. I let others know that I was timidly hopeful for the future of blacks in South Africa. I wasn't going to go overboard with joy at this one positive occurrence. Being ever pragmatic, I took more of a wait-and-see approach.

Although Mandela had been released from prison, I did not feel that economic sanctions should be loosened. South Africa had mistreated the majority of its people for decades, and I was not persuaded that the country had been reformed by the release of Nelson Mandela. To me, South Africa needed to prove that it had reformed before any action was taken to offer economic reward or relief to this country.

MeToo/TimesUp

Similarly, today women and racial minorities in this country cannot allow their pursuits of equality to be dismantled. The MeToo and TimesUp movements, for example, are equality movements that must persist and persevere until the final victories on sexual assault, harassment, and inequality in the workplace are won. Women and minorities cannot be mollified by pyrrhic victories. There is simply too much at stake. Power yields grudgingly, and it must be taken by persistent nagging.

Rainbow Coalition

After he announced his candidacy for President, Jesse Jackson came to Des Moines and asked to meet with community leaders. Given that I served in the senate, I met this standard. Jesse and I talked one-on-one, and I decided to support his campaign. Later, his Iowa co-chair, Evelyn Davis, a local community activist, advised me that Jesse was returning to Des Moines to campaign. She asked if he could host a meeting at my house, and I consented. It was a fantastic meeting. Jesse sat in the middle of my basement and regaled a crowded basement with his knowledge and commentary on the issues. He is a truly gifted speaker, and I was thrilled to be able to host him in my own home.

Along with Evelyn Davis, I co-chaired the Jesse Jackson statewide campaign for President in Iowa in 1988. In this role, I presided over Jackson's meetings at the County Convention and the statewide Democratic Convention. I also led the Jackson delegation to the Democratic National Convention in Atlanta, Georgia. After the National Convention, Jesse Taylor and I returned to Iowa to spearhead the Iowa Rainbow Coalition.

I worked on the Rainbow Coalition during Jesse Jackson's campaign. The purpose of the Rainbow Coalition was to increase voter turnout in the polls by registering new voters for the upcoming election. In July of 1988, about 500,000

Iowans were eligible to vote, but not registered. The coalition worked to change that. I felt that black and other minority candidates should fare better in Iowa because of the coalition. While my work as a senator and lawyer took up most of my time, I put in as many hours as I could during the campaign.

NAACP

In 1990, the NAACP recognized my accomplishment as being the first black to be elected to the state senate in Iowa. I am stated as saying I appreciated the distinction in being recognized by the NAACP as Iowa's first black senator but that I took no pride in it, as it took more than one-hundred-and-thirty-five years to occur, and I was the only black senator in the state. I wanted other African Americans who had served in the legislature to be remembered. I did not want their legacies to be forgotten.

In my view, black needs are human needs, and human needs are black needs. If you solve the problem for one subset, you solve it for the other. While in the legislature, I fought for human needs. I also represented black constituents statewide. I was the only black legislator in Iowa, although there had been other blacks in the house, including Willie Glanton from Des Moines, Al Garrison from Waterloo, William Hargrave from Iowa City, and Melville Peter Middleton from Waterloo.

Many of our victories in the long struggle for justice for blacks in this country have come through the courts, which is why I first wanted to become an attorney. Indeed, when we could not win justice in the political process, we have resorted to the courts. And that was true over one-hundred-and-thirty years ago in Iowa when a slave by the name of Ralph came to Iowa from Missouri with the written permission of his white owner. Ralph was sent to Iowa to earn money working in the lead mines of Dubuque. Ralph's owner sought to reclaim him, and in 1839, the Supreme Court of the Territory of Iowa ruled that Ralph was a free man under the laws of the Territory of Iowa. This was an enlightened ruling as compared with the 1856 Dred Scott Decision of the U.S. Supreme Court, wherein that court ruled that blacks were property, mere chattels, and not entitled to any rights under the laws of the United States.

On-the-Job Stress

While I enjoyed the work during both of my senate terms, I also found the job to be quite stressful. I was experiencing increasing symptoms of agoraphobia and anxiety, such as stress and excess sweating, along with stomach issues, including ulcers and sour stomach. It was the resultant agoraphobia and attendant symptoms that exacerbated my stress as I worried that others would notice.

But I loved the work, and I loved politics. I was finally passing legislation that could make an impact on people's lives. Leala and I discussed my concerns before I ran for my second term. We discussed whether I should run, as I was starting to experience increased feelings of anxiety before speaking on the senate floor. But my love for the job and Leala's encouragement caused me to stick it out for a second four-year term. Unfortunately, I was speaking out on key issues on a daily basis while we were in session, which exacerbated the symptoms and made things pretty unbearable for me toward the end of my second term.

Chapter 10

Moving On

To thine own self be true.
— William Shakespeare

A Sort of Dissonance

Over the course of my two terms in office, it became clear to me that the stress of being a public servant who was under constant scrutiny and who had to challenge those in positions of authority conflicted with my being a black man who was raised to be meek and subservient to authority figures. This daily conflict and resultant stress were taking a toll on my health, as my symptoms of agoraphobia and stomach issues continued to worsen.

I do not know what the total impact of the overt racism that I grew up under had on me, but I do know that I had the same doubts and insecurities that many people have as I fought to make a future for myself and my family in Iowa politics. Ever since I was a young boy in Tennessee, I had been conditioned to follow instructions and to not challenge those in positions of authority. As I began to make my way in my legal career, it became clear that I would have to challenge others, including authority figures, on a regular basis. This was not easy for me. It created a sort of dissonance that affected me on a deep, psychological level, which also started to manifest physically.

I was raised to follow directions without questioning them. On one occasion when I was in the fourth grade, my second cousin and teacher, Sarah Waller, let our class know that she had to leave for a bit. She told us to stay in our seats while she was out. I don't know how long she was gone, but it seemed like a very long time. Unfortunately, while she was away, I needed to go to the bathroom. Because she said we had to stay in our seats, I fidgeted, trying not to move or get out of my seat. Unfortunately, because she was gone so long and I did not want to disobey her, I soiled my pants.

This one event has had an emotional impact on the rest of my life, linking my stomach to anxiety and stress. When Ms. Waller returned, she was sympathetic and did not scold me. Instead, she sent me to the restroom with my Uncle Alfred so he could help me get cleaned up. However, when the students from my class came into the restroom and saw what happened, they laughed and made fun of me in the restroom and again later that day on the bus ride home. Ever since that incident, I have suffered from bowel problems, which are aggravated by stress. During my second senate term, I began to have some understanding of the connection between this event, which led to my eventual leaving of the senate in January of 1990.

White Knuckles and Self-Care

I had great difficulty coping with the stress of being in public office. For the most part, I just "white knuckled" my way through it, but it was excruciating and something that I had to deal with daily. No matter how difficult it got, though, I just put one foot in front of the other and kept pushing forward. During my second senate term, Leala and I would often discuss the toll that being in public office was having on me and whether it was in my best interest to leave the senate.

After many discussions, we decided it would be best to complete my second term. However, I did seek help from my personal care physician as soon as it was apparent that I was having stomach issues. At the time, I was having great difficulty with stomach gas. My doctor tested me and told me that I was lactose intolerant. Unfortunately, changing my diet didn't resolve the issue. So, I sought help through biofeedback treatments. I used a Greg States tape to learn biofeedback so I could semi-relax, but that didn't fully solve the problem either.

After that, I started seeing a physician at Methodist Hospital in Des Moines. Under this physician's care, I visited the Mayo Clinic in Minnesota. While at the Mayo Clinic, I was subjected to every reasonable test that they knew of, but they, too, were unable to find a solution to my issue. As a result, they concluded that I probably had a small ulcer and encouraged me to modify my diet to give my stomach some time to heal.

Unfortunately, a change in diet was not sufficient to alleviate all of the debilitating symptoms I was experiencing. When I was having major problems with agoraphobia and perspiring under my arms and staining my suit coat jackets in Judiciary Committee meetings, I looked for a way to relieve the pressure. I thought perhaps if I could reduce my workload a bit that would help. So, I asked Senator Douglas Ritsema, a Republican from Orange City, if he would serve as chair of the subcommittees on some of the bills that were under my review. In the meantime, I could work other bills through the Judiciary Committee, but he declined. Unfortunately, compromise with the Republicans was often difficult, even when it came to small favors.

Making It Official

My symptoms had grown so intense during my second term, I came close to quitting several times before the end of the term. On one occasion, I had drafted my resignation speech to give on the senate floor. Reverend Henry Thomas of Union Baptist Church in Des Moines gave the invocation that morning on the senate floor, and he and a group of senators, including Senator Hutchins, Senator Horn, Senator Riordan, Senator Welsh, and Senator Murphy, talked me out of it after the service. On another occasion, Senator Hutchins talked me out of it after I privately expressed my concerns. I also had many conversations with Leala about my discomfort at going to work and, like my colleagues, she encouraged me to stick it out each time we discussed it.

However, sticking it out created a vicious cycle for me: I would worry over the physical symptoms, which produced more of the physical/feared symptoms, which, in turn created more worry and more physical symptoms. During the second half of my second senate term, I sought additional help to obtain relief from the physical and psychological symptoms I was experiencing. Since changing my diet and biofeedback weren't helping that much, my physician put me on Klonopin, which helped ease some of the anxiety I was experiencing.

Once I decided I would stay on for the rest of my second term, I wanted to come clean and share what I was going through, in case it could inspire others to seek help for similar conditions. On February 21st, 1998, an article in the *Des Moines Register* came out on the agoraphobia and pressure I was experiencing from being in the public eye. In the article I shared, "You're just bombarded with requests for audiences all the time. … In my case, I am constantly in the settings that I fear."

The article shed light on the effect that my constant fight for justice and having to look whites and people of authority in the eye while debating them on key legislative issues was having on my health. It also shared how this was in direct opposition to my upbringing and how this was manifesting physically as ulcers, sour stomach, halitosis, and flatulence and mentally as agoraphobia. The article also offered hope to readers by sharing that help was available for these conditions.

The Call to Serve

Almost a year after the article that came out in the *Des Moines Register*, I decided to make my decision to step down after my second term public so that other aspiring senators could start preparing their campaigns. It was a hard and carefully considered decision to not seek a third senate term. But once I announced to the press on December 20th, 1989, that I would not seek a third term, I felt less pressure and stress overall.

In my statement to the press I explained, "While serving as state senator, I have tried to meet the great demands placed on me as an elected official, and as a black elected official. I have tried to be an effective spokesperson for justice and equality. And I have tried to meet my obligation to be a role model and to make race work for black people and other minorities, and not against them. I feel that I have accomplished these goals. So, it is with great reluctance that I announce I will not seek re-election. ... I believe that it is important that Iowa's leadership reflect the cultural diversity which exists in the state. And so I encourage both major political parties ... to identify and recruit minority candidates for public office."

I was at ease with my decision to go public with my retirement and to invite other leaders to step forward and to continue the work I had begun in the senate. I still had my law practice, and I intended to continue practicing law after my senate term ended. Not that practicing law was without its own levels of stress. I had many rough days in the courtroom, but I was confident that I had made the correct decision, given how I was feeling at the time.

And while early in my career I always thought I would run for higher office, ultimately the side effects of my condition would preclude that. I had hoped that revealing my problem to the public would relieve some of the pressure. However, the problem was deeply ingrained, and a run for higher political office was not to be.

An Outpouring of Support

I worried that I would get a poor response from my colleagues after the article came out about my condition and I publicly expressed my intention to retire after my second term, but they were very sympathetic. Many colleagues urged me to stay the course and sent me kind notes and letters. I was deeply relieved and gratified by each of the letters I received. They alleviated some of the pressure that I was feeling at the time. It was such a comfort to know that I was not alone and that others understood what I was going through.

I was particularly pleased to receive a letter from Representative Ralph Rosenberg, a Democrat from Ames, who expressed regret over my retirement and of not being able to work with me directly in the state senate. Ralph was a good friend of mine, and his support meant a lot to me. We had discussed the possibility of the two of us running for governor one day. I always thought that he had a better chance of being governor than I, and he thought the same of me.

I was also heartened to receive a note from Congressman David Nagle who shared that he had enjoyed working with me and that he was disappointed to hear that I was stepping down. David and I had worked together when he was Chair of the Democratic State Central Committee and I a Central Committee member.

I received a note from Senator David Readinger, a Republican from Urbandale. Senator Readinger had shown me great sympathy and understanding while we served together. I would occasionally express some of my frustrations about my agoraphobia to him. He was a good listener, and he also supported my MLK Day celebrations and gave me a copy of Dr. King's "I Have A Dream" speech.

I also received a letter from one of my constituents, Sophia Katz, which touched my heart. Sophia suffered from anxiety, and she wanted me to know that we were in the same boat and that she would not judge me for my condition. There were many other letters from legislators, expressing their support. My reveal to the media had partially accomplished its purpose: I was already feeling a sense of relief and inspiring others who had similar afflictions.

In an article dated April 13th, 1990, in *The Des Moines Register*, I spoke to the widespread practice in Iowa of electing local governing boards to seats representing an entire community, which makes it difficult for black candidates to succeed. At the time, my district was twelve percent black, which meant African American candidates were going to have to sell their platforms to a white majority based on their ability to do the job. The article shared that I was the only black out of one-hundred-and-fifty state lawmakers, which made my decision to not see a third term a reluctant one.

Looking back, I probably could have hung on for another four years and served a third term. I was unopposed in the last election and chances are I would have won a third term. But my health was the factor that ultimately caused me to retire early. By sharing my condition and my decision to retire with the public, the end of my second term gave me a sense of closure.

I was ambitious, and had I been healthier, I would have stuck it out. But I have no regrets. I received a great amount of support from my family and colleagues and had a decent career as a lawyer, which enabled me to stay true to my life's path and goal of helping those in need while making a difference in society by setting standards of conduct for employers and corporations in each legal case that I took on.

Retirement Honors

Iowa Senate

In May of 1989, the night that I acknowledged my retirement from the senate, I was almost brought to tears by the praise and support that my senate colleagues extended to me. They knew I had been suffering and could have been silent or judgmental. Yet, they were not. Their kind remarks and the commendations that I received in the following days truly warmed my heart.

In the weeks after my speech, I received many notes and letters from my colleagues. I read each letter that they had sent and took the time to write everyone back, thanking them for their support and for having been so thoughtful and understanding when I gave my speech. Senator Bill Hutchins announced his deep regret over my retirement in his senate memo to Democratic staff, dated December 19th, 1989.

Former Colleagues

In addition to letters from senators and congressmen, I also received letters from those I had worked with prior to joining the state legislature. In each letter, I began to learn how much I had touched peoples' lives in my service to Iowa.

I received a letter of support from Alfredo Parrish who said I had been a "tremendous asset to the state of Iowa" and that he was sorry to see me leave the senate. Al and I had repaired our differences from our ICRC days. There was a mutual respect between us. He was a great lawyer, and I a struggling politician.

I also received a nice note from Charles Palmer, director of Human Services, thanking me for my public service. I had worked with him when I was an assistant attorney general when I represented the Mental Health Agencies and the Department of Corrections, and again in the senate when I served on the Appropriations Committee for Mental Health and Corrections.

I was pleased to receive a sympathetic note from Sue Follon. Sue had been executive director of the Iowa Commission on the Status of Women when I was director of the ICRC. It was great to know that she was still in my corner. I also received a nice note of support from Janice Harris. Janice had worked for me at the Civil Rights Commission. I had lost track of her after leaving the ICRC. It was so heartwarming to hear from her after so much time had passed.

Justice Arthur McGiverin, Chief Justice of the Iowa Supreme Court, sent another kind note, expressing appreciation of my support of the judicial department. I had handled the court reorganization bill and other bills of interest to the court, and I appreciated his recognition and support.

I also received a note from Jim Carney who had lobbied for the Iowa Bar Association. He was very helpful to me. He even explained the difference between a "sharecropper" and a "tenant farmer" to me one time. I came to know from his explanations that a sharecropper lives in Tennessee and a tenant farmer lives in Iowa. In his note, he shared, "The real purpose of this letter is not to share another copy of the resolution, but to tell you that I will miss you, the Bar Association will miss you and all the lawyers of the State of Iowa will miss you at the Capitol next year. Your service in the Iowa senate was a statement of professionalism."

U. S. Senator Tom Harkin sent me a very nice note, thanking me for my contributions to the senate and my service to the state of Iowa. I knew Senator Harkin from the campaign trail and Democratic politics. I also had testified before his subcommittee on Labor, Health, and Education. Senator Harkin wrote a bill for the disabled at the national level, and I think he would have made a fine president.

A note from Tom Slockett, Johnson County Auditor, was received. His words gave me more proof that I had been heard across the state of Iowa and that there was statewide support for the work I had been doing. Additional support came in the form of a note from Patricia Geadelman, director of Governmental Relations, University of Northern Iowa, who stated, "You have served with distinction, and your presence will be missed. Your moral leadership, presiding skills, and good humor will be especially hard to replace. I wish you well in whatever pathways you choose for the years ahead." I was heartened by her words and grateful that my work to increase educational opportunities for minorities in the state had made a difference.

Black History Month

The black caucus of the Iowa Democratic Party honored my retirement on February 25th, 1990, during their Black History Month Celebration. I gave short remarks at this event and was pleased to receive the honor being bestowed upon me. During my remarks, I borrowed from Proverbs 22:1 to the effect that, "A good name is to be chosen rather than great riches, and favor is better than silver or gold." I was appreciative of the good name being bestowed upon me by the black caucus.

It surprised me that the audience was given notepads to write thank-you notes to me at the event. I was very pleased to receive these notes afterward. I was particularly pleased to receive a note from Tom Parkins, the chair of my campaign, and his wife Judy Fitzgibbon, the chair of the Des Moines Civil Service Commission. In his note, Tom shared that one of his proudest moments was when I was elected to the Iowa State Senate. I fought back tears as I read that because it was also one of mine.

I was glad that John Roeherick, Chair of the Democratic Party, had sent a note and stated that he would try to "carry some of the load on civil rights and civil liberties" issues. I read through a note from Evelyn Davis, my co-chair of the statewide Jesse Jackson campaign, and it touched me that she remembered our work together and wanted to express her gratitude in that way. It was a very special night, and I still hold onto the memories (and handwritten notes) from this event.

1990 Civil Libertarian of the Year Award

It was a high honor to receive the Iowa Civil Liberties Union's Civil Libertarian of the Year Award in May of 1990. This was a fair reflection of the work that I had done in the state legislature. I tried to be a humanitarian as well as a civil libertarian, and I took this as evidence that I succeeded in doing both.

The award was presented in Iowa City, Iowa. I remember driving about two hours to Iowa City the day of the award and driving home immediately afterward. Even though the event ran long, I couldn't stay overnight, because I was having a major problem with agoraphobia and its attendant symptoms by then.

U. S. Senator Charles Grassley, a Republican from Iowa, inserted remarks in the Congressional Record at the gracious request of State Senator John Jensen, a Republican from Plainfield. In his remarks, Senator Grassley said, "I rise today to salute one of the great leaders in advocating civil rights and justice in the State of Iowa: Mr. Tom Mann, who is retiring after serving eight years in the Iowa State Senate. ... I congratulate and commend Mr. Mann on his exceptional accomplishments and service to the people of Iowa." While Senator Jensen and I were philosophically opposed, I really appreciated this expression of respect from him and Senator Grassley.

Stand Up and Be Counted

On June 3rd, 1990, I was honored on my retirement from the state senate. Around fifty people attended the tribute at the Des Moines Community Hall as part of the second annual "Stand Up and Be Counted" weekend, which was sponsored by the state's black caucus. Leala and I attended the celebration. At this event, the Democratic party leaders referred to me as a "man of compassion, persistence, and conscience whose leadership, particularly among blacks, will be deeply missed." Members of the audience echoed each other, as they offered their support and praise for my work.

At the event, I thanked the organizers and the community for their support. I appreciated their approval of my work as, like most individuals, I operated better under a spirit of approval rather than dissent. At the event, I received very high praise from members of the black caucus. Deborah Turner, an assistant professor at the University of Iowa's College of Medicine offered, "The reason we could stand up and be counted is because Tom Mann stood up and was counted before us."

I am always a little bit uneasy whenever someone says something nice about me. However, I was pleased to receive public support from the audience. I told those in attendance that I was a "reluctant quitter." They cheered as I added, "If you really want to pay tribute to me, then bust your butts between now and November to elect a Democrat. Put people in office who will pursue the same goals and aspirations that I have pursued."

It was a bit of a bittersweet moment for me as I reflected on my retirement from the senate at the event. Fortunately, I knew that I had my law practice to keep me going, and I looked forward to continuing to serve others as a private attorney in the years ahead.

Post-Retirement

As many are aware, politics is not for the timid. It is a rough sport. At the same time, it is a beautiful way to contribute to the community, and I do not regret my decision to serve in public office or my decision to leave when I felt it was time to step down.

Retiring from the senate ultimately did not completely relieve my stress and anxiety. I still face stomach problems and agoraphobia today, and I'm convinced that both will follow me to the grave. However, with the use of medication and relaxation techniques, I can function and was able to continue with my life's work until I retired from practicing law for the state government of Texas in January of 2016.

Chapter 11

A New Pace

Granma said when you come on something good, first thing to do is share it with whoever you can find; that way, the good spreads out where no telling it will go.
— Forrest Carter, The Education of Little Tree

Friends and Family

After retiring from the senate, I took it easy for a while. I spent time with my family and friends and visited the law office during the week and on Saturdays. After hours, I relaxed by inviting my fraternity brothers and family over to play poker. James McCown, Zack Hamlett, Gary Wilcots, Jessie Currie, and Jeffrey Currie became some of the regulars who came for poker night. We'd have big gatherings at our house where Nari would hang out while we played pool and poker. Nari, ever wanting to be included in any activities, soon joined in on the fun. On her insistence, I taught her how to play chess and poker. We would practice on the poker table in the basement. I sat her on my knee and taught her how to play five and seven card stud. Sometimes, she would pretend to be the teacher and tell me to "play my cards close to my chest." When we were playing chess, I made sure Nari knew the name of each piece. She was in awe as she watched the pieces move on the marble chess set. She was a fast learner and enjoyed being included in on the fun. Nari enjoyed playing chess so much that Leala bought her a young adult book called

The Jose Gambit. We'd also put together jigsaw puzzles together on the poker table. Nari found it comforting how each of the pieces fit together.

It was good to be home more often and to be spending time with my loved ones. The girls were taking tap and ballet classes and would perform for an audience each summer in a yearly recital. They were also taking bowling lessons around this time. Leala would take them to their dance and bowling lessons. I remember they really enjoyed the bowling lessons and even had their own bowling balls to take with them. All four of us went bowling on occasion, which was fun for us all. Leala and I wanted to show our support for the girls, so we took time out for recreation whenever we could. Overall, we kept busy, me and Leala with work, and the girls with school and extracurricular activities. It was a happy time for us.

When I was a senator, I had been working about seventy-five hours per week, which was a more challenging pace for me. After my retirement from the state legislature, I cut my hours back to about forty-five to fifty hours per week. Initially, I was working more hours in my private practice, but I learned to reduce my hours back to a more manageable rate by training myself to work fewer hours each day so that I would have more time to spend with family and friends.

Eventually, I got used to the new pace of working just one job. In the summer of 1990, I even took a two-week road trip to South Dakota with my cousin, Jeffrey Currie. We drove through the Badlands and saw rock formations that developed from calcified trees. On our trip, we visited Mount Rushmore National Park and saw the granite faces depicting U. S. Presidents George Washington, Thomas Jefferson, Theodore Roosevelt, and Abraham Lincoln. We also visited Deadwood, South Dakota, where we played poker at Kevin Costner's casino. It was a fun trip, one that allowed me to decompress from the usual stresses at work.

Back in Des Moines, I continued to work on Saturdays. Nari and Kari would often join me in the office where they had ample toys to play with and books to read. I also had a portable TV that they would sometimes watch. If the girls had a school project, they may have also worked on it at the office. Homework, on the other hand, was to be done in a timely manner at home right after school or any extracurricular activities, so it was rare that they would be working on homework at the office, unless it was a special assignment that took more of their time.

Leala would also join us on Saturdays. It was her day to catch up. The girls were still pretty young at this time. Kari was in first grade, and her sister Nari was in fifth grade. I remember one weekend Nari took the WordPerfect tutorial on one of the office computers. She enjoyed learning how to type and how to use the word-processing software. I was impressed with her facility for computers as well as her interest in the program and her ability to pick it up so quickly.

In my office, I had a framed portrait of Dr. Martin Luther King behind my desk, right over my head, and Nari mistook it for me one day. I chuckled at Nari's suggestion and explained that it was not a drawing of me but of a great civil rights leader. I relayed that he was an important person and that, although I was laughing, I was touched that she mistook him for me.

I spent the nights at home with Leala and the girls. And, as was my custom, I would read to Nari and Kari in the evenings before bed. Nari was growing older and becoming very curious about the world around her. After seeing how well she took to the WordPerfect tutorial at the office, Leala and I decided to buy her a desktop computer to use for her homework and class projects. She loved her computer and went on to become a computer specialist, which was a source of pride to me and Leala.

Nari was a fast learner and a good student. Kari was a good student, too, but she was more reserved and shier than her older sister. Nari liked to play Tetris on her computer, and she would often beat me when we played together. One day when we were playing, Nari mentioned that Peter Tchaikovsky wrote the music for Tetris. I smiled and was proud to learn something from my daughter that I hadn't known previously. Her thirst for knowledge and attention to detail ran deep. She subscribed to *Nintendo Power* magazine and became a video game aficionado. It was fun father-daughter time.

Nari and I would also watch TV and movies together. She was especially fond of comedies starring John Candy and Dan Aykroyd and anything by Mel Brooks, so I would bring home lots of movies for us to watch together from Blockbuster. I also got her a book of lawyer jokes when she was in elementary school. She would recite the jokes to me and make me laugh. Over time she developed a lifelong love of comedy and even did some standup for a while when she got older.

When we watched TV, Nari paid close attention to the shows as well as the commercials and would sometimes question the products we used in our home. Once she asked why we used Dawn dishwashing liquid when Palmolive was better, according to the commercial. I laughed at the innocence of her question and explained that commercials were not always to be relied upon as truth. I explained that the claims in this commercial were those of the company and not necessarily the consumer. It was a tactic to get more people to buy their product. She nodded her understanding as we watched the rest of the program. Over time, she would question other products and came to learn more about the correlation between advertising and consumerism.

Private Practice

Wrongful Termination

The caseload in my private practice was keeping me pretty busy. On March 6th, 1986, I worked on a wrongful termination case where I filed suit for a client who alleged that he had been discharged from employment by his employer, which was in violation of his oral contract. My client also stated that his employer intentionally cut his tenure on the job short, which violated their verbal contract. I saw this as a wrongful discharge that went against public policy.

The case was starting to take a rather circuitous route. On July 29th, 1987, the Clerk of the County District Court issued a notice that stated the case would be dismissed if we didn't go to trial by January 1st, 1988. I responded to the notice, letting the clerk know that I filed a certificate of readiness for trial on behalf of my client on August 11th, 1987. The employer, however, resisted, asserting that they needed more time to do discovery, and the trial court rescheduled the pretrial conference for October 12th, 1987.

On October 12th, 1988, I filed a motion for summary judgment. The trial court, however, did not issue its ruling on the motion until after January 1st. As a result, on January 6th, 1988, the trial court issued its ruling, denying my client's motion for summary judgment. And on January 8th, 1988, two days after the judge's ruling was filed, the clerk entered an order dismissing the case for not timely pursing a trial. Unfortunately, I did not receive a copy of the order, and the parties continued to pursue this case as if it had not been dismissed.

On July 7th, 1988, I filed a motion requesting the court to rule on legal issues that would resolve the case. On July 15th, 1988, the trial court entered an order, refusing to rule on the motion, noting the case had been dismissed. I then filed a motion to reinstate the case. The employer resisted, and the trial court denied the motion to reinstate the case. I then appealed to the Iowa Supreme Court, and the court ruled in his favor. The case was returned to the trial court, and in 1991, I was able to negotiate a settlement for the sum of $150,000.

Workplace Discrimination

I also worked on a high-profile workplace discrimination case. The plaintiff was an Iranian Muslim who worked for a large auto parts company. On October 17th, 1988, the plaintiff filed a complaint with the Iowa City Human Rights Commission, alleging that he had been discriminated against by his employer on the basis of color, national origin, race, and religion. He complained that he had been subjected to racial slurs and insults, including the terms "camel jockey," "terrorist shiiat," and "shit-head Muslim," among others. One defendant admitted that terms like these were in common use at the company. The Iowa City Human Rights Commission (ICHRC) ruled that probable cause existed, which was in favor of the plaintiff's claims that he had been discriminated against. The ICHRC then tried to resolve the complaint by conciliation, which failed.

The plaintiff, in turn, filed suit against the company on January 19th, 1989, alleging that discrimination on the basis of race in employment had occurred. The trial began on September 16th, 1991 and continued through October 2nd, 1991. It ended in victory for the plaintiff, with the court awarding him around $15,000 in damages, plus $50,000 in attorneys' fees.

However, most of my cases ended in settlement with a confidentiality, non-disclosure agreement that expressed that the parties would not disclose anything from the case to current or former employees of the company or to any members of the general public or news media, except when necessary to implement its terms and conditions. Plaintiffs were also allowed to disclose the agreement to immediate family members, legal counsel, tax preparers, or as directed to do so by a court or other judicial agency. Since the lawsuits, which gave rise to these settlements, were public records and had been the subject of prior news reports, the parties could disclose that a dispute between the parties existed and that the dispute had been resolved, without disclosing the details of the settlement.

Texas

In the summer of 1991, Leala and I began to discuss moving to Texas. Leala did not like the cold winters in Iowa, and she had family in Texas, which made her want to return home. Her father was living in Killeen, and her mother was living in Buda, so we decided to move to Austin, which was right between the two. We moved in late 1991. I drove the blue Cadillac until we moved to Texas, when my brother, Kenneth Maclin, gave me a classic Mercedes Benz, which I drove for a while. While I loved my brother and appreciated the gesture of giving me such a nice car, a part of me missed that old Cadillac.

In 1991, Leala and I bought a four-bedroom house in Hunter's Chase. The family that was living in Iowa did not follow me to Texas as they had when I first moved to Iowa. My mom and many of my extended family members stayed behind in Iowa. I still had family in Tennessee as well, and once we moved to Texas, we frequently saw Leala's mom and stepdad, Alberta Vaughn and Troy Vaughn. We saw Leala's dad, George Salter, Sr. My mom also came to visit us and ended up staying with us in Austin for a while. It was nice having her around, and the girls, who had grown attached to my mom when we lived in Iowa, loved having their grandma so close by.

Nari had many friends in Iowa and had great difficulty adjusting to the move. She grew somewhat rebellious during this time. She had been scheduled to attend the Gifted and Talented Students classes in Des Moines and was disappointed that we were moving because she was looking forward to the classes. She said that all she knew about Texas was "Yosemite Sam," adding that she didn't like him.

After the move, Leala and I went to work and returned home one day to find that Nari had started painting her bedroom purple. The damage was done, so we finished painting it purple with her, but we also grounded her for four weeks for changing the color of her room without consulting us first. The punishment worked, and the purple room was the last room she ever painted in the house.

Fortunately, after that Nari started to settle into her new life in Austin. She made new friends and also met Sonya Hamilton, who would become her lifelong best friend. Kari was more neutral about the move and adjusted pretty quickly. The girls had started dance lessons back in Des Moines and resumed their tap and ballet lessons when we moved to Austin. They also took gymnastics, and Nari played the piano. They both enjoyed dance and going to the pool with Leala, and Kari actually grew into a very good swimmer. She swam in some tournaments and won lots of ribbons, which she displayed in her room. In her class of swimmers, she had placed second or third, which made her very happy. And in my spare time, I taught the girls how to ride bikes, which they rode around their new neighborhood with their friends.

Occasionally, we visited my family in Tennessee. Usually we would go for the Fourth of July or Christmas. I always took Leala and the girls with me because I wanted them to see where I had grown up and for them to know their extended family. We also went to Brownsville, Tennessee, to attend our family reunions. These were held every four to five years. Family from Des Moines and Tennessee would be at these reunions. We'd either stay at my Grandmother Carrie's house or with my Uncle Fragia Maclin who lived close by.

We had great feasts at the reunions. My mom and my aunts Annette and Arnette were great cooks. We usually ate brown beans, collard greens, ham, chitterlings, pork chops, corn bread, potato pies, cakes, and sometimes pig feet. The girls weren't picky eaters and had a great time hanging out with their aunts and uncles and cousins and eating everything we put on their plates. After we stuffed ourselves, the adults would gather and play cards, and the kids would entertain themselves with games like hide and seek. I have fond memories of these reunions, which continue to this day.

Texas Commission on Alcohol and Drug Abuse

Leala and I were admitted to the Texas State Bar and to practice before the Texas Supreme Court on March 5th, 1993, after taking the Texas Multi-State Bar Examination. Leala and I took the exam at the same time. We had spent about two months studying and preparing our applications, usually in the evenings when the girls were sleeping. The state required background information, letters of recommendation, and other certificates of good standing, so the applications we submitted were about fifty pages in length. I also was admitted to practice before the United States District Court for the Western District of Texas on April 8th, 1997. I submitted letters of recommendation and certificates of good standing as a basis for admission to this court.

In September of 1993, I found a position with the Texas Commission on Alcohol and Drug Abuse. I worked at the Commission for just over two years. During this time, I advised commissioners and the administration on legal questions concerning the agency. I also helped agency personnel interpret and apply the law whenever it pertained to the agency and prepared legal opinions as requested. In addition, I rendered opinions by interpreting and reviewing drafts of laws, rules, and regulations that affected agency operations and administration. I also prepared drafts of bills and proposed amendments to agency regulations and represented the agency in administrative hearings.

I worked at this job for two years until I was fired. Texas Governor George W. Bush was unhappy with the agency and wanted to put it in receivership. In my view, it was a political move. I filed suit for wrongful discharge, and in April of 2000, I signed a settlement agreement with the state of Texas. The settlement entitled me to a sum of $180,000, which covered all claims for damages, equitable relief, attorney's fees, and costs associated with this litigation. Before the agreement was signed, I practiced law and worked for the Texas Railroad Commission in 1997 and 1998 where I pled and processed complaints against polluters of the oil fields and participated in administrative hearings for the commission.

Des Moines

After moving to Austin, I visited Des Moines about four times to wind down my law practice and to visit with family. I tried one case in federal court in Cedar Rapids that involved an African American man named Byron Curry. Mr. Curry began working for the Illinois Central Gulf Railroad on April 23rd, 1979 as a brakeman. In 1985, a man by the name of John Haley began to negotiate to purchase the portion of the Illinois Central Gulf Railroad known as the Iowa Lines where Mr. Curry worked. The Iowa Lines consisted of approximately seven-hundred-and-five miles of track from Omaha to Chicago, including a line to Sioux City and Cedar Rapids. By December 24th, 1985, the purchase was completed, and the Chicago Central & Pacific Railroad came into being and was authorized to operate.

By the terms of the Purchase and Sale Agreement, the Illinois Central Gulf Railroad was required to deliver a list of five-hundred-and-fifty of its employees to the Chicago Central

& Pacific Railroad within thirty days of the agreement. Chicago Central was, in turn, required to make each of their employees resign under the condition they would be rehired by the new company, Chicago Central. Chicago Central agreed to offer employment to the employees on the basis of seniority as set forth in the Rail Line Employee List, which was subject only to the buyer's rights to reject any employee for reasonable cause and up to fifteen employees without cause.

Byron Curry, like other employees of the former railroad company, signed the resignation form and applied for employment with Chicago Central. Mr. Curry, unfortunately, was not offered employment. The case was tried and all evidence was taken. The court did not make a finding but issued a strong suggestion that the case be settled outside of court. A confidential settlement was reached after the trial.

Private Practice

I specialized in civil rights cases in my private practice from 1995 to 1997. During this time, I interviewed clients and witnesses, investigating to determine whether we had a case. I also did discovery, which entailed serving requests for additional information and taking depositions. In addition, I prepared exhibits and other pretrial work, mediated cases, and did trials before the courts and administrative agencies.

Leala and I set up a joint law practice in 1998, which we named Mann and Mann, after our practice in Des Moines. At Mann and Mann, which we ran until 2003, I was engaged in a limited practice doing civil rights cases. My duties included interviewing clients and witnesses, investigating claims, and doing discovery. I also handled some family law cases, whereas Leala focused on family law and bankruptcy.

Applied Materials

One case that I took on in my private practice involved an African American gentleman named Roy W. Bradshaw who started working for Applied Materials on March 22nd, 1993, as a shipping clerk. Mr. Bradshaw eventually worked himself up to an analyst position. He performed this job well and received performance evaluations, which documented his performance and good work. In June of 2000, he applied for a promotion to the position of buyer and was assured by Paul Lackman, his manager at the time, that he would get that job.

While Mr. Bradshaw was qualified to do this job, he was not promoted. He was told by Mr. Lackman, a Caucasian male, that he did not get promoted because he had misplaced Mr. Bradshaw's paperwork. Mr. Bradshaw stated the job was instead given to Peter Aills, a Caucasian employee.

Around September of 2000, Mr. Bradshaw's position as an analyst was ending. He was then given the job of planner I, which was another entry level position. On or about September 13th, 2001, he received his annual performance evaluation. At this time, Mr. Bradshaw asked his supervisor, Ted Morales, a manager at Applied Materials, when he would be promoted. His supervisor told him that he would need a bachelor's degree to get promoted. Mr. Bradshaw recalled that over ten white employees who did not have bachelor's degrees at the time of their promotions had been promoted. And some of these employees were now supervisors and managers, with Bradshaw having trained some of them.

I filed suit on behalf of Mr. Bradshaw in 2001. The defendants filed their response on December 20th, 2001. The defendants asserted that the parties had agreed to submit all controversies arising out of the employment relationship to arbitration and that an agreement to arbitrate was enforceable under federal law. The defendants contended that the Federal Arbitration Act required that the agreement be enforced, and the district court agreed. On April 22nd, 2002, Mr. Bradshaw demanded that arbitration be held.

On November 27th, 2002, the arbitrator ruled against Bradshaw on all issues. Ordinarily, the next step would have been an appeal. But because this was an arbitrator's award, an appeal would not have been productive. During the hearing, the court ruled in his favor on all of the evidentiary issues. So, there were no legal challenges that could have been raised based in the hearing. As a result, we did not pursue the appeal.

Other Texas Employees

Texas Railroad Commission

In addition to my private practice, I continued to work for some Texas employers. From 1997 to 1998, I was appointed as a staff attorney at the Texas Railroad Commission where I pled and processed complaints against polluters of the oil fields and participated in administrative hearings.

Texas Workforce Commission

From 2003 to 2004, I worked as an administrative hearing officer with the Texas Workforce Commission where I researched laws, regulations, policies, and precedent decisions to prepare for administrative appeal hearings in unemployment compensation cases. I conducted hearings to discover facts bearing on appeals in accordance with federal and state laws and procedures regarding unemployment compensation in the state of Texas. I also questioned witnesses and ruled on exceptions and motions and the admissibility of evidence and adjudicated eligibility issues raised in appeals filed by claimants and employers.

In 2004 until my retirement in 2016, I worked as an assistant manager of the Special Hearings Department with the Texas Workforce Commission. In my new role, I researched laws, regulations, policies, and precedent decisions to prepare for administrative appeal hearings involving unemployment tax liability decisions, career school cases, child labor law cases, and Texas payday law cases. I also conducted administrative hearings to discover facts bearing on appeals in accordance with federal and Texas laws and procedures and questioned witnesses and ruled on exceptions, motions, and the admissibility of evidence. As the assistant manager of the Special Hearings Department, I also supervised other hearing officers and administrative staff.

Retirement

Pro Bono Work

I retired from my position at the Texas Workforce Commission on January 29th, 2016. Although I am officially retired, I still take on occasional pro bono work and also write wills for people. As far as politics go, I make occasional donations to political campaigns and to the Democratic Party. And I still follow politics closely, but from a distance, which is a more comfortable spot for me these days.

Some of the pro bono I have worked on since my retirement includes:

2017

- I worked on a case for client who was seeking unemployment benefits. The issues were whether the claimant had good cause for quitting work and whether the claimant committed misconduct at her prior employment. I represented the claimant at her unemployment hearing, and she won her benefits.

2018

- I worked for a client who was contesting the application for a Protective Order in a divorce case. I worked out a settlement with the county attorney, which included a Protective Order.

- I worked on another case for a client that involved speeding and a DWI charge. I worked out a plea bargain agreement that allowed the client to continue his freedom, pay a fine, and do community service in lieu of going to jail.

- A third case I worked on involved back taxes owed to the Internal Revenue Service (IRS). I worked out an agreement that included an Offer in Compromise with the IRS, and the client was able to pay a minimum, affordable amount.

Leala

Leala also had a successful legal career. She worked for the Texas Department of Transportation, the Texas Department of Aging and Disability Services, and our joint law practice. She retired in 2010 to help Nari when our daughter was having some health issues. Leala and I had discussed the matter, and she decided she would retire early so she would have more time to be with Nari. Since our retirement, we have enjoyed having more time to spend with friends and family. Leala and I have both had long and fulfilling careers, and we're now appreciating this next phase of our lives as we continue to share our experiences with the next generation, in hopes that they can carry on the work we began.

Chapter 12

Family Values

A promise must never be broken.
— Alexander Hamilton

The Importance of Family

I still remember when Nari learned to ride her bike when we were living in Iowa. It was a moment of pride for both of us.

"Daddy, Daddy! I'm doing it! I'm riding my bike! Can you see?" I smiled proudly as Nari pedaled her pastel-colored bike in the Woodlawn Elementary School parking lot near our Iowa home in 1985. It warmed my heart to see her pedaling so furiously, determined to cover as much distance without training wheels as she possibly could.

I nodded and waved my approval as she rode in circles around me. Leala and I had been working with Nari to help wean her off the training wheels over a period of several weeks. Her friends were starting to ride without their training wheels, and Nari said she wanted to ride like the "big girls" in her neighborhood. The training wheels were adjustable, so we loosened them little by little to give Nari the opportunity to practice wobbling between the two wheels. The last ride we went on, the wobble was pretty substantial, and Nari did great. I told her that I thought next time we could take the training wheels completely off. Nari, ever the achiever, was excited that I thought her day to remove the training wheels had finally arrived.

The next day she watched as I removed the training wheels and set the kickstand down so she could mount safely. "You ready?" I asked. Nari nodded eagerly. I smiled. "I'm going to hold on for a while so you get the hang of it, OK?" Nari looked straight ahead, determined, as she kicked up the kickstand and gripped the handlebars, "OK, Daddy. Let's go!"

We started off slowly, I held the back rim of her bike seat, walking alongside my daughter as she steadied herself. After a while she started to pedal faster, and I jogged to keep up. Soon after, I released my grip on her seat and continued running beside Nari, who hadn't noticed I was no longer holding onto her seat. She started to pedal faster, and I stopped to catch my breath and soak in this moment with my daughter, who shouted excitedly when she realized she could ride her bike without any training wheels or help from me.

Nari spent countless hours riding her bike with her friends after she achieved this milestone and became a very good cyclist that summer of 1985. A few years later, she went on a bicycle camping trip with her Girl Scout troop and earned the bicycling badge, which she wore proudly all summer. She tells me that she is grateful for how I supported and steadied her throughout her life in moments like these so she would have strong wings to fly with on her own, while also learning the importance of returning to the family "pond" so she could stay connected to her roots.

I grew up with a large extended family. We often lived under the same roof. From an early age, I learned that family was important, and I wanted to extend this teaching to my daughters who also grew up with the blessing of having family and close friends around. According to my eldest Nari, "Growing up, the importance of family was something that was understood. We had family come to visit. We, in turn, would go visit our family. No one was ever turned away. We even had friends and relatives living with us for extended periods of time until they could find a place of their own.

My mom and a host of brothers and other relatives lived in our basement for a while when we lived in Iowa. It was important to me that my girls learned the importance of family. I lived this value then and still do today. According to Nari, "Family was important to my development. I love my extended family and am grateful to my dad for teaching me this."

The Value of a Good Education

I decided that I wanted to be a lawyer so I could help others by making important decisions that would affect people's lives in a positive way. I also dreamed of becoming a politician so my legislative decisions would have an even greater reach/impact on others. This is why I went to college and studied law and eventually ran for state office while living in Iowa.

Because I felt it was important to carry on this legacy of helping others, I urged both of my daughters to become lawyers. They rejected this advice, however, and would not entertain the suggestion. Nari, ever fond of computers, became a computer specialist, which was her own way of being of service, and my youngest, Kari, always sensitive to the needs of others, became a physical therapist so she could help people recover from a range of injuries. Looking back, my advice took. It just took a different route, and I am proud of both of them for entering into helping professions that resonate with their own natures.

As far as teaching our girls about money, while the girls were not given allowances, Leala and I tried to impress upon them the value of money, regardless of the amount, and how they should be grateful for whatever gift they were given because it was an act of kindness from someone else. To this day, Kari is careful about money, but Nari still has to be watched.

I remember one time when we were at the ballpark in Des Moines Nari found a penny in the dirt near home plate. I was playing softball with some friends. I watched as she picked up the penny and threw it in a trash barrel. I stopped what I was doing to teach her the value of money and why she should not throw away something as small as a penny. Nari said she didn't consider a penny to be money. I chuckled and reminded her of how my family struggled to make ends meet when we were kids, and I was taught to be frugal and that even a dirty penny was worth having. I wanted to impress that point upon Nari who, in turn, dusted off the penny and put it in her pocket as she watched the rest of the game. As I resumed playing on the field with my friends, I watched Nari closely. She would take the penny out of her pocket from time to time, to study it, and then carefully place it back in her pocket, taking care not to drop it. I was pleased that she had understood my teaching, which I hoped she would carry with her throughout her adult life.

The Importance of Being Kind to Others

I give of my time and efforts generously, especially to those less fortunate than me. Nari and Kari learned from me and also give generously to others. Leala and I weren't necessarily lenient parents, but we were far from strict. We fell somewhere in the middle, as far as discipline went, and tried to guide Nari and Kari into being good and decent human beings. As part of this training, they both had chores to do before they went off to school so they would learn the importance of community and helping others. They were taught to make their beds and put away their dishes in the dishwasher and to clean up after themselves in general. With a little help and nudging from me and Leala, they did all of their chores before heading off to school each day.

The girls did not typically fight. I remember only one fight in Des Moines, and Nari remembers one in Austin. They were taught by me and Leala not to fight, and this lesson took. They maintain cordial relations to this day and make sure to spend time together, whenever they can. As a family, we still travel together. We have taken several trips and cruises together. On our last cruise, we went to the Caribbean in December of 2012. We cruised on the Carnival Magic around Christmas that year. We visited Montego Bay, Jamaica; Georgetown, Grand Cayman; and Cozumel, Mexico. We spent three days at sea and had a blast. We had a balcony suite and ate great food and enjoyed our time at sea. Leala, Kari, and Nari went snorkeling when we were in Jamaica while I toured the island. Leala and the girls took an enjoyable trip to Hawaii in May of 2019. They chose Hawaii because Leala has been wanting to go for a long time. While they were away, I caught up on my reading and worked on my author website.

As the eldest child, I have been designated the family patriarch. I take this title seriously and wanted my daughters to learn the importance of being kind and generous with others by leading by example. As the patriarch of my extended family, people look to me for guidance and leadership in matters involving the family.

My daughters remember this going all the way back to our time in Des Moines. Because of my stature in the community and my savvy about legal matters and politics, family would always come to me for advice, resolution of quarrels, financial or legal assistance, and direction in matters involving the whole family. I am touched that my daughters remember these events and that they have learned the importance of giving to others. To me, this is the most shining and undying example of kindness and love. It is the most salient lesson I can think of teaching to my girls. And it was one that I didn't really have to explain. I showed them by living this value and being of service to friends and family in need.

I remember when famine was a big focus in the eighties and there were movements like Band Aid and Farm Aid. On Sunday music days with Leala, we would listen to the song "We Are the World." I remember one day when Nari was very young, she was sitting in the dining room with me and Leala eating her breakfast. At the time her favorite breakfast was Quaker Oatmeal. As we ate and listened to the song, I tried to explain to Nari that not everyone had all the things like food and security that she had. Leala and I explained the significance of the song, and I remember Nari looked down at her bowl of oatmeal, her most prized breakfast offering, and asked if she could send some of her oatmeal to Africa. Leala and I were touched that Nari wanted to donate her breakfast. We smiled and told her that she could keep her breakfast and that we would donate some money so the children in Africa could buy their own oatmeal, if they wanted. Nari seemed pleased with that and resumed eating her oatmeal as we continued to listen to the song.

Leala and I also demonstrated kindness by using reasoning to discipline, rather than spanking, our children. Once I had to tell my mother not to spank Nari. I told her that we used grounding and timeouts to discipline our children to help them learn the reasoning behind the punishment, rather than disciplining them with corporal punishment, which was something we wanted to avoid. Leala and I would always take the time to reason with our girls and speak to them with respect, as if they were adults, so they would learn the concepts and values from our point of view, rather than just blindly punishing or domineering them.

When I was in the Legislature, I co-sponsored a bill prohibiting corporal punishment. The bill's lead sponsor was Joy Corning, a Republican from Cedar Falls. Julia Gentleman, a Republican from West Des Moines, was another sponsor. The bill passed the senate 32-18 on March 2nd, 1988 but died by failing to pass both houses by the legislative imposed deadline of March 26th, 1988. I am happy to report that the bill was revived in 1989 and was passed into law in May of 1989.

The Importance of Honoring Your Word and Commitments

I also taught both our girls that "your word is your bond" and that it is important to honor your commitments. I spent most of my professional career working to get others to honor the commitments they had broken. Unfortunately, I do not think that it always stuck at home. I was called upon to remind Nari of this principle just this week, who was backing out of her commitment to spend time with my cousin Jeff Currie, who was scheduled to come to Austin to visit us. Leala had wondered aloud if he might not come earlier that week and Nari stated that she wasn't planning to visit if they came. I reminded Nari that our word is our bond. I told her that, if Jeff said that he would be coming to Texas, he would show and that she should plan on spending time with him when he was in town. She understood and said she misunderstood Jeff when she was speaking with him on the phone because she thought he was wanting to explore the city on his own and that she was not trying to get out of spending time with them. Jeff and his wife Katherine showed how we honor our commitments in this family, arriving to visit us soon after the discussion I had with Nari. In turn, Nari was able to make amends and spend time with my cousin and his wife during their visit. I was pleased that she had learned this lesson and that the values I had worked hard to instill in my daughters were taking hold.

Afterward

Racism is still with us. But it is up to us to prepare our children for what they have to meet, and, hopefully, we shall overcome.

— *Rosa Parks*

Much progress has been made in race and gender relations in this country since the time that I was a boy growing up in Tennessee. There has been nothing less than a revolution in race relations. Laws have been changed to prohibit discrimination on the basis of race and sex, and for that I am grateful.

The Civil Rights Act of 1964 prohibited discrimination on the basis of race, creed, color, religion, and national origin in employment and public accommodations. In 1965, the Voting Rights Act was adopted. And on September 24th, 1965, President Lyndon Johnson issued an executive order requiring government contractors to take "affirmative action" to hire without regards to race, creed, color, or national origin. As a result, the majority of this country is no longer of the view that, as stated by the United States Supreme Court in 1856 in the Dred Scott Decision, "a black man had no rights which a white man was required to respect."

The laws affecting minorities in this country have changed. However, as stated by the court in Bakke v. Regents of the University of California in 1976, "...although legal impediments to equality have been removed by the judiciary and by the congress...minorities still labor under severe handicaps. To achieve the American goal of true equality of opportunity among all races, more is required than merely removing the shackles of past formal restrictions: In the absence of special assistance, minorities will become a 'self-perpetuating group at the bottom level of our society who have lost the ability and the hope of moving up.'"

We've had meaningful and substantial change, and we can continue to pursue a "more perfect union" by not shrinking from progressive polices that promote women, racial minorities, and the LGBTQ community. I used to tell my staff at the ICRC that we would never be able to work ourselves out of business. But we could bring justice to those who brought claims before us. And we did. And I encourage those of you in positions of power to do the very same today.

Today, we are fortunate to have a field of good Democratic Party candidates for president. I like all of those who are running. Any one of them would make a fine president. If given the opportunity, I will support Senator Kamala Harris and former Congressman Beto O'Rourke as a single ticket, with Senator Harris in the 2020 presidential spot. This pairing would bring a common-sense perspective to the presidency on issues such as climate change, healthcare, and civil rights. They are progressive candidates who could best achieve social and economic equality for our country, and I wish them the greatest success in the upcoming debates and primaries.

Life taught me to pursue a good education, so I could get ahead and make a difference in this world. When I pledged for the Omega Psi Phi Fraternity in college, I was taught that we must all persevere. As Aristotle said, "All who have meditated on the art of governing mankind have been convinced that the fate of empires depends on the education of youth." H. G. Wells added that, "The difference between catastrophe and history is education." These are sentiments that I support. I firmly believe that education and perseverance were the keys to any success I have had in my life and that these keys also extend to anyone who is willing to pursue them.

As I shared with the Iowa youth and minority voters when I worked in the state legislature, voting is essential to bringing about the necessary change that this country needs. Everyone who is eligible to vote must be allowed to and make the effort to vote. Voting is not just a privilege; it is an obligation. Voting in large numbers during presidential elections can also overcome any drawbacks in the electoral college.

Young Americans of voting age have an obligation to vote. Too many people in this country have paid a heavy price, including bludgeoning and death, to fight for the right of minorities in this country to vote. Moreover, voting is the best way for any group of citizens to be heard and to make the government responsive to their concerns.

I am of the opinion that every single vote should have equal weight and not be diluted by a system such as the electoral college that allows our president to be chosen by anything less than all votes cast. Legislation has been introduced in Congress to abolish the electoral college. It will require the assent of at least thirty-six states. If you, like me, wish to abolish the electoral college, you can help make a difference by doing the following: First, request that your members of Congress support the legislation. Second, request that your state legislators support the legislation. We live in a representative democracy; therefore, you should take the initiative and ask your legislators to represent your views.

As I reflect on the events that have occurred since the last presidential election, I can see that President Trump has worked diligently to undermine our democracy, but he is not alone. Senate Majority Leader Mitch McConnell, a Republican from Kentucky, has made a major contribution to this phenomenon, as have other Republicans in Congress. These Republican leaders have either assented or silently gone along with Trump and McConnell, which makes them complicit not only in the continuous strain on our democracy but also on the party's inevitable destruction.

Right-wing media and other arms of the Republican party have done a great deal of damage to our democracy as well. These arms of the Republican party spread distortions and outright lies. On April 11th, 2019, for example, Fox News reported that Donald Trump had an approval rating of fifty-five percent, which was simply not true. Trump had an actual approval rating of forty percent. On the same date, *The New York Post* used a partial quote of Congresswoman Ilhan Omar, a Democrat from Minnesota, about the 9/11 attacks on New York City. The article attacked Representative Omar and put her life in jeopardy. Like the Fox News report, this article was pure distortion.

These lies and distortions by the right-wing media and pundits hurt and imperil our democracy. A democracy depends upon a free and honest press. A free and honest press is important to maintaining an informed electorate, which is the lifeblood of any democracy. These efforts to misinform the citizenry strikes at the heart of our democracy, and I fear that the effects will be long-lasting, if not permanent. Given the First Amendment and our right to free speech, transparency is the only solution. The press and common citizens must call out these acts of betrayal and gaslighting coming from the administration and rebuke the right-wing media at every turn.

When I worked as an assistant attorney general for the state of Iowa, I was faced with the question of whether Native American inmates at the Fort Madison prison could build and worship in a sweat lodge on the prison grounds. Their plan was to bring in a shaman to lead their worship services. I was asked for my opinion as to whether this should be allowed, and I supported this request. After much debate, it was allowed. I share this and other stories in this book with you not to boast about my accomplishments, but rather to share how taking steps to promote civil liberties in this country can have positive outcomes for those seeking change. I call upon you, regardless of your position in life, to follow in my footsteps and to seek out causes that speak to you so that you can take action to make your world a better place for others. Together, a step at a time, we can make a difference.

Author Q&A

1. What made you decide to write this book and what do you hope this book will accomplish?

I retired from public service in 2016. In looking for ways to fill the time, I decided to write about my life and convey to family, friends, and the public the hardships that I suffered, the triumphs that I enjoyed, and the obstacles that I evaded throughout my life. I hoped to inspire and encourage others to seek their goals, whatever they may be. Coming from where I started, I had little outward hope of becoming a lawyer and public servant. Yet, this was my dream and my quest, and I made it happen. In writing this book, I wanted to convey to others that with hard work and determination they can make it, too.

2. What was it like growing up in the Jim Crow South and seeing signs like the ones above water fountains and restrooms with "Whites Only" and "Colored Only"?

It was demoralizing. To have people look down on you, to require that you look up to them, and to constantly remind you that you were being treated as a second-class citizen was horrible. It robs a person of their dignity and sense of self-worth. The stress of living under those conditions lead to mental and physical health problems, such as the ones that I suffered.

3. Some readers, particularly those with privilege, may not fully grasp the lasting psychological damage that segregation and the unspoken code of conduct for African Americans during the Jim Crow

era has done to minorities in this country. Can you shed some light on that for this demographic and how this unspoken code is still in effect today?

As mentioned above, the effects of living under constant racism leads to mental and physical health problems. This is a continuing problem for me. When I worked at the ICRC, I was always impressed with the fact that we could not work our way out of business as a commission. There was always more discrimination. There is always more discrimination and more work to be done.

4. What sort of conversations did you have with your daughters about your upbringing and what you wished for them when they grew into adults?

I have told my daughters repeatedly about how I grew up. They have actually grown tired of hearing it. I grew up on a farm, poor, and without advantages, and this they know. But I did not let it stop me from achieving my dreams. I told them that they can do whatever they desire to do. And that it will just take some hard work and perseverance to make it happen.

5. In your memoir, you spoke of the importance of getting a good education and how doing so enabled you to fulfil your life's dream of practicing law and serving in the state legislature. What would you say to today's minority youth who may feel discouraged or unable to attend college due to the rising cost of education in this country?

I would share that they do not have to go to Harvard, Stanford, or Yale. There is always another option. Elizabeth Warren, 2020 Democratic candidate for president, attended community college at fifty dollars per course. She then went on to become a Harvard professor. As I told my daughters, anything is possible, provided you work hard and persevere.

6. What do you think it is going to take to address the systemic racism in this country today? Moderate politicians have been able to effect slow, gradual change since the sixties, but, as you state in your book, there is still much work to be done. Do you think it is a matter of being patient? Or should we elect a liberal populist president to effect quick and radical change to create a more fair and equitable society for others? Or is a hybrid politician more in order—someone who can communicate well with both parties while also taking steps to implement a more fair and progressive agenda for minorities?

I say rip the band-aid off and solve the problem now. I'm not for going slow. Minorities and women have been going slow for four hundred years. It is now time for change.

7. What would you say to today's youth who feel discouraged by the current political climate? And what advice would you give them on effecting positive change in this country?

Young people today are already active, and they should remain so. I am heartened by the high schoolers that marched for climate change just a couple of weeks ago, and the students from Parkland, Florida, who championed gun control in 2018. I would say to the young people, "Keep it up."

8. In your memoir you mention some moments when you were discriminated against, including having your acceptance letter to practice law in the state of Tennessee rescinded, not being served in a restaurant while you were a state senator, and being shown dilapidated houses when you and your wife first went shopping for your first home in Iowa. Can you share with the reader what these situations were like for you and what you would say to anyone who experiences similar discrimination today?

The above incidents were not the only incidents of racism that I have experienced in my life. When you grow up under a regimen of racism, some acts become routine and are not catalogued, so I wanted to share a few of them in my memoir to give the reader a sense for what I was up against. For those who encounter this type of racism, I would say be strong and fight back. In your own way, discover that inner strength so you can stand up for yourself and for others.

9. Are you still in touch with some of your colleagues from the Iowa senate? If so, how often do you speak or visit?

I am not in regular contact with members and former members of the Iowa Senate. Biannually, the Iowa General Assembly sponsors the Pioneer Lawmakers Assembly where former lawmakers get together. I drove to Des Moines and attended the assembly in 2017 and had an opportunity to meet with other lawmakers who served with me in the senate. It was a great pleasure to chat with my former colleagues. Arriving at the hotel, I came upon Senator William Dieleman, a Democrat from Pella. We walked into the hotel together. When we got inside, I spoke with Senator Jean Lloyd-Jones, a Democrat from Iowa City. I also met up with my good friend Senator Carr who rode back to the capitol with me.

When we arrived at the capitol, I came upon Senator Larry Murphy, a Democrat from Oelwein, Senator Gene Fraise, a Democrat from Fort Madison who is the current chair of the unofficial "burial committee," and Senator Hutchins, a Democrat from Audubon. We were served a luncheon, which I ate in the company of Senator Hutchins and Senator Leonard Boswell, a Democrat from Davis City, who left the senate after three terms and served in the U.S. Congress until 2012. At the event, I also met with former speaker Donald Avenson, a Democrat from Oelwein, and Representative Wayne Ford, a Democrat from Des Moines.

There were many others in attendance, including members of the media, and I enjoyed seeing them all.

10. In your book you mention the importance of family, and it seems that in spite of your busy schedule, you always seemed able to carve out some time to spend with family, such as when you visited your brother Keith in the hospital when you ran for senate the first time and the time that you spent reading to your daughters at night, often at the end of a very long workday. Can you share with the reader why family is so important to you, sharing why these moments are seen more as moments of joy rather than obligation?

I grew up in a large extended family. We were a close-knit family, the kind that looked out for each other. I loved that feeling and looked forward to preserving it within my own nuclear family. I encourage the same kind of relationship for my daughters. To this day, I still feel that closeness with my extended family.

11. You have also written a novella titled *Surveillance* about a character that was illegally surveilled during a high-profile civil rights case. What inspired you to write this story and do you think something like that could happen today?

Surveillance is a book that grew out of my own experiences. The book takes place in Texas, but in actuality, it is inspired by events that took place when I was practicing law in Iowa. In the book, I relay a number of experiences that caused me to believe that I was under surveillance. While much of the work is fictionalized, the undercurrent of invading privacy and surveilling others is a very real threat we face in today's high-tech society.

About the Author

Growing up in the Jim Crow South and witnessing the discriminatory practices against African Americans in his community, Thomas Mann, Jr. knew at a young age that he wanted to become an attorney and a legislator so that he could work to improve the lives of minorities in this country. Tom was the first person in his family to graduate from college, earning a bachelor's degree in political science from Tennessee State University in 1971 and a juris doctorate degree from the University of Iowa in 1974.

After passing the Iowa State Bar exam in June of 1974, he began working as an assistant to the state attorney general where he argued criminal appeals cases before the Iowa Supreme Court and represented the Iowa Civil Rights Commission in ongoing discrimination cases. In November of 1982, Tom became the first African American to be elected to the Iowa State Senate where he served two consecutive terms. While a state senator, he served as Vice-Chair of the Senate Judiciary Committee, Chair of the Business & Labor Relations Committee, Chair of the Ethics Committee, and President Pro Tempore of the Senate. After his tenure in the state senate, he continued his work as a civil rights attorney, where he fought for civil liberties in the states of Iowa and Texas until his retirement in 2016.

Newly retired, Tom has taken up writing. He also takes on the occasional pro bono case and enjoys spending time with his family. He lives in Manor, Texas, with his wife, Leala, and his two daughters, Nari and Kari. *The Call to Serve* is his second book. To learn more about the author, visit www.thomasmannjr.com.